The Fulcrum
of the Entire Universe

Isaiah 53:
The Pivot Point of All history

By Dr. Chuck Missler

Koinonia House

The Fulcrum of the Entire Universe
© Copyright 2017 Koinonia House Inc.
Published by Koinonia House
P.O. Box D
Coeur d'Alene, ID 83816-0347
www.khouse.org

Author: Dr. Chuck Missler
Editor: Amy Joy

ISBN: 978-1-57821-697-0

All Scripture quotations are from the King James Version
of the Holy Bible.

PRINTED IN THE UNITED STATES OF AMERICA

Table of Contents

Chapter 1
The Book of Isaiah

The Dead Sea Scrolls were first discovered in late 1946 in caves along the Dead Sea. The ancient settlement of Khirbet Qumran held millennial old sealed clay jars that contained about 1200 manuscripts, including more than 300 Biblical texts. Arguably the greatest discovery at Qumran is the Great Isaiah Scroll, a nearly complete scroll that was copied around 125 BC. It contains all 66 chapters of Isaiah.

In this book, we will focus on a particularly interesting passage in the second half of Isaiah: chapter 53. It has been called the Holy of Holies of the Old Testament. These twelve verses offer a summary of the entire New Testament, written more than 700 years before Jesus Christ was born. A number of passages in the Hebrew Scriptures describe the victory of the Messiah as the ruler of the world, and the Jews have focused on those. This chapter provides another unexpected purpose for the great King; it's an incredible prophecy that describes the Messiah as a servant who suffers and dies for His people.

Isaiah's Writing

The Book of Isaiah opens with a declaration of its authorship. In verse 1:1, the prophet Isaiah, son of Amoz, states that he wrote his prophecy during the reigns of "*Uzziah, Jotham, Ahaz, and Hezekiah, kings of Judah.*" Chapter 6 of Isaiah describes a vision that took place "in the year that King Uzziah died," – about 740/739 BC.[1] Isaiah volunteers to be a prophet in this passage, and the LORD gives him a dismal task:

> *And he said, Go, and tell this people,*
> *Hear ye indeed, but understand not; and*
> *see ye indeed, but perceive not. Make the*
> *heart of this people fat, and make their*
> *ears heavy, and shut their eyes; lest they*
> *see with their eyes, and hear with their*
> *ears, and understand with their heart,*
> *and convert, and be healed. Then said I,*
> *Lord, how long? And he answered, Until*
> *the cities be wasted without inhabitant,*
> *and the houses without man, and the land*
> *be utterly desolate, And the LORD have*
> *removed men far away, and there be a*
> *great forsaking in the midst of the land.*
>
> Isaiah 6:9-12

Throughout Isaiah, the heart of God cries out to the hard-hearted people of Judah. He alternates back and forth between rebuke and comfort, rebuke and comfort. Meanwhile, Isaiah offers some of the most profound prophetic passages in all of Scripture, describing the future sometimes years, centuries, and even millennia in advance.

The majority of Isaiah gives us a rich variety of poetry. Wisdom poetry and hymns of rebuke, prediction and prophecy pour at us from chapters 1-35. We then find a change in pace at chapters 36-39, where Isaiah turns to prose. During this "bridge," the prophet gives an interesting historical narrative describing important events during the reign of King Hezekiah. Then, at chapter 40, the poetry of comfort, prediction, and rebuke picks up again until the end of the 66 chapters.

Right in the center of this second part, we find the focus of our present study: Chapter 53. It is located 13 chapters from chapter 40 and 13 chapters from chapter 66. The Bible's chapter divisions were not in the original; they were placed in the New Testament in the 13th century AD and in the Hebrew Old Testament in the 15th century, but the chapter breaks often follow thematic breaks in the text.

I like to follow the *Holman Bible Commentary* and further divide chapters 40-66 into three parts:[2]

- The Purpose of Peace: 40-48
- The Prince of Peace: 49-57
- The Program of Peace: 58-66

The second subsection on The Prince of Peace is bookended by essentially the same verse. Isaiah 48:22 states, "*There is no peace, saith the*

LORD, unto the wicked." Isaiah 57:21 repeats this sentiment, saying, "*There is no peace, saith my God, to the wicked.*" This gives us natural section divisions:

- The Purpose of Peace: 40-48
- "No peace for the wicked" 48:22
- The Prince of Peace: 49-57
- "No peace for the wicked" 57:21
- The Program of Peace: 58-66

In the middle of this second section, we find chapter 53. I'm calling it the Fulcrum of the Entire Universe. That might sound a bit heady, but this passage truly is the pivot point of all history. While Isaiah 9:1-7 or 11:1-10 describe the glorious future reign of the Messiah, this powerful chapter toward the end of the book gives a much different picture. Here we find the Messiah as a sacrifice who suffers to pay for the sins of the people.

The two ethnic roots of Judaism are actually divided over Isaiah 53. The Ashkenazi Jews were so disturbed by this chapter that they removed it from their Bible altogether. The Sephardic Jews thankfully left it in. When the Dead Sea Scrolls were found, the Great Isaiah Scroll included Isaiah 53 with all its unhampered power. What's more, it dates to the second century before Christ was born, demonstrating the existence of these verses in the book of Isaiah long before Jesus entered history and died.

The Israeli Museum has a special building dedicated to the Great Isaiah Scroll, and Isaiah

53 cries out from it. The original book of Isaiah was written over the course of Isaiah's adulthood between 740 and 686 BC, long before many of the events it describes in advance occurred. This passage is so important that it is cited in all four Gospels as well as Acts, Romans and 1 Peter.[3] What makes it so important? The crucifixion of Jesus Christ.

Crucifixion

We know that crucifixion was not invented until the Persian Empire, after which it was widely adopted by the Romans.[4] The official form of execution in Israel was stoning. It's particularly startling, therefore, to find the crucifixion of the Messiah detailed in Isaiah centuries before this form of execution was invented.

Psalm 22 is another important passage that describes Jesus' death from the viewpoint of Christ hanging on the cross. His unbroken bones, His thirst, His pierced hands and feet, His humiliation and ridicule, and even the gambling done for His clothes are all described by David in Psalm 22, nearly 1000 years before the crucifixion took place. Zechariah 12:10 adds to the picture, declaring, "*They shall look upon me whom they have pierced,*" offering a description by the LORD of those who will see Him at His return.

Here in Isaiah 53, we find the purpose of Christ's death written centuries in advance. Isaiah is a supernatural book, and this is a supernatural passage.

Deutero-Isaiah

> *Who hath believed our report? And to*
> *whom is the arm of the LORD revealed?*
>
> Isaiah 53:1

It is popular these days to split Isaiah into two parts, crediting the authorship of the first 39 chapters to Isaiah, son of Amoz, and chapters 40 to 66 to an entirely different person (Deutero-Isaiah), who lived hundreds of years later. The first part of the book is seen as a series of warnings and rebukes made by the original Isaiah, while the last part is seen as a series of comforting passages made by Deutero-Isaiah after the Babylonian captivity.

It is a fact that the Book of Isaiah describes events that took place long after the death of Isaiah, son of Amoz. Secular historians and Bible critics have dismissed these prophetic passages as written after the fact. They do not recognize Isaiah's divine inspiration; they presume that somebody else wrote those prophetic verses after they took place.

Hastings Bible Dictionary quotes biblical critic A.B. Davidson's summary of secular thought about prophecy:

> *The prophet is always a man of his own time and it is always to the people of his own time that he speaks, not to a generation long after, not to us. And the things of which he speaks will always be things of importance to the*

*people of his own day, whether they be things
belonging to their internal life and conduct,
or things affecting their external fortunes as
a people among other peoples.*[5]

Isaiah doesn't obey A.B. Davidson's ideas about
the purposes of prophecy. He doesn't just prophesy
to the families of Judah, and he doesn't just speak
to the people of his day. He cries out the words
of God to the many lands surrounding Judah –
and unto the whole world.[6] He declares that he
speaks to future generations:

*Now go, write it before them in a table,
and note it in a book, that it may be for
the time to come for ever and ever:*

Isaiah 30:8

Isaiah prophesied from about 740-686 BC.
The Kingdom of Israel in the north was conquered
by the Assyrians in 722 BC, and we find in Isaiah
36-37 that the Kingdom of Judah nearly suffered
the same fate. God protected Judah from its
enemies because faithful King Hezekiah of Judah
trusted in the LORD. It would take several more
generations for Judah and its capital at Jerusalem
to fall to Nebuchadnezzar of Babylon in 586 BC.

Yet, Isaiah does not focus much on Assyria,
the enemy of his day. He repeatedly speaks of
the future, about the rise and fall of Babylon.[7]
He describes long in advance the ascent of the
Persian Cyrus the Great, whom the LORD

calls by name in Isaiah 44:28-45:6. *"That saith of Cyrus, He is my shepherd,… That they may know from the rising of the sun, and from the west, that there is none beside me. I am the LORD, and there is none else."*[8]

Through His prophet Isaiah, the LORD constantly speaks of the distant future. He does this as a sign of His eternal power, because He knows the stubbornness of His hearers:

I have declared the former things from the beginning; and they went forth out of my mouth, and I shewed them; I did them suddenly, and they came to pass. Because I knew that thou art obstinate, and thy neck is an iron sinew, and thy brow brass; I have even from the beginning declared it to thee; before it came to pass I shewed it thee: lest thou shouldest say, Mine idol hath done them, and my graven image, and my molten image, hath commanded them.

Isaiah 48:3-5

There are a variety of external and internal facts about Isaiah that point to a single author.[9] Jewish tradition has always attributed the book to Isaiah alone, and in the Dead Sea Scrolls we find the Great Isaiah Scroll has no division at all after chapter 39. It is a single large scroll, completely credited to Isaiah, son of Amoz. In his book *The Unity of Isaiah*, Oswald Allis jokes, "Obviously the scribe was not conscious of the alleged fact that an important change of situation, involving an entire change of authorship, begins with chapter 40."[10]

The writing of Isaiah is among the best, most beautiful and skilled poetry in all the ancient world. This excellent writing skill continues from chapter 1 to chapter 66. What's more, we see no Babylonian influence in his vocabulary. In the post-exilic books of Esther, Ezra or Nehemiah, we find a range of Babylonian vocabulary and idioms, but Isaiah contains only pure pre-exilic Hebrew.

The subject matter in both halves of Isaiah is rebellion and idolatry, problems that had passed away after the Babylonian exile. The land of Israel described in Isaiah is the rocky, mountainous land of Israel and not the wide, flat land of the Fertile Crescent.

> *And they shall go into the holes of the rocks, and into the caves of the earth, for fear of the LORD, and for the glory of his majesty, when he ariseth to shake terribly the earth.*
>
> Isaiah 2:19

> *Enflaming yourselves with idols under every green tree, slaying the children in the valleys under the clifts of the rocks?*
>
> Isaiah 57:5

Isaiah constantly calls God, "The Holy One of Israel" throughout his entire book. It's a name used in only six verses by other Bible writers. Isaiah uses it repeatedly, 12 times in chapters 1-39 and 14 times in chapters 40-66.

There are only a couple of reasons to split up Isaiah between two or more writers. The first is a distinct bias against predictive prophecy. Those who doubt God's existence and deny His power will not accept the reality that God is the First and the Last, "*Declaring the end from the beginning, and from ancient times the things that are not yet done.*"[11] They refuse to believe that God spoke to Isaiah and told him things in advance. They therefore attribute the prophetic passages to other writers.

A misunderstanding of the purposes of prophecy might be a second reason to split up Isaiah. There are those like A.B. Davidson who force the prophet into a narrow box, relegating his words to the small groups of people around him. These critics will not accept that Isaiah wrote to distant peoples and future times, and they will feel obliged to credit other writers with Isaiah's words to broader audiences.

Taken at face value, however, the internal and external evidence point to a single Isaiah who saw the throne room of the LORD and spoke to all of us from the heart of the eternal Godhead. We should not be surprised that Isaiah sometimes offers stern rebuke and then turns and speaks with comfort. His words are communicating to us from God, who hates the sins of His wayward people, but who loves them and longs to heal them just the same.

Bible critics invented "Deutero-Isaiah" for their own purposes, without solid evidence. It's frankly irrational to suggest that one of the greatest, most skilled writers of all time just vanished from history. There was never even a hint of any other writer until modern scholars declared they knew better. Well before the time of the New Testament, all understood that Isaiah had written the entire book.

> *Who hath believed our report? And to*
> *whom is the arm of the LORD revealed?*
>
> Isaiah 53:1

This is the first verse of Isaiah 53, and John quotes it in Chapter 12, verse 38 of his Gospel. He notes that the people didn't believe Jesus even though He performed many miracles before them. He then quotes Isaiah 6:10, reminding us that the LORD told Isaiah their eyes would be blinded and their hearts hardened:

> *Therefore they could not believe, because*
> *that Esaias said again, He hath blinded*
> *their eyes, and hardened their heart;*
> *that they should not see with their eyes,*
> *nor understand with their heart, and be*
> *converted, and I should heal them.*

*These things said Esaias, when he saw
his glory, and spake of him.*

John 12:39-41

In one breath, John quotes from Isaiah 53, and in the next breath he quotes from Isaiah 6, crediting both to Isaiah.

It's interesting that John quotes from the first and last parts of Isaiah in two breaths, attributing them both to Isaiah without any question. As a teenager, I ran into this, and I now regard John 12:39 as a treasure. That verse saved me hours of tedious library research. Here John cuts through it all. The Isaiah who wrote Isaiah 53 and the Isaiah who wrote Isaiah 6 are the same Isaiah, and those who do not believe are simply hardened. John is telling us – and the entire Bible is telling us – that there is only one Isaiah. Knowing this will save us all a lot of money buying nonsense commentaries that deny the power of God.

Chapter 2
The Messiah

The death of the Messiah the Prince was predicted in Daniel 9:26. In his famous 70 Weeks prophecy, the angel Gabriel tells Daniel that the Messiah would be cut off - כרת - *karath*. The term *karath* means to be killed and indicates execution for a capital crime:

> *And after threescore and two weeks shall*
> *Messiah be cut off, but not for himself: and*
> *the people of the prince that shall come*
> *shall destroy the city and the sanctuary;*
> *and the end thereof shall be with a flood,*
> *and unto the end of the war desolations*
> *are determined.*

Daniel 9:26

Gabriel told Daniel that the Messiah would be executed, but not for himself. Daniel grew to adulthood during the Babylonian captivity, after Jerusalem and Solomon's Temple had been demolished under Nebuchadnezzar. We get a simple order of events in Daniel 9:25-27. The city and its wall would be rebuilt during troublesome times. The Messiah would be executed, but not for himself. Then the city and Temple would be destroyed again.

The post-exilic books of Ezra and Nehemiah describe the rebuilding of the Temple and Jerusalem. The Gospels detail the public ministry and execution of the Messiah, and Josephus tells us that the city and Temple were destroyed by the Romans in A.D. 70 during the First Jewish-Roman War.[12]

Gabriel's prophecy was not a new one. Long before Daniel, Isaiah had already described the sacrifice of the Messiah.

The Messiah in Isaiah

We find that the Isaiah 53 passage actually begins three verses earlier at the end of chapter 52. Remember that the Old Testament chapter divisions were put in place in the 15th century; they were not in the original. They simplify the process of finding specific verses, but the divisions themselves cannot be considered inspired. Let's back up and read through, look at the lead-up that we find in Isaiah 52:1-12.

Koinonia Institute sponsored the translation of Isaiah directly from the Great Isaiah Scroll (Dead Sea Scroll) by the foremost expert on the scrolls, Dr. Peter Flint, for use in the International Standard Version (ISV). I will offer the ISV in parallel to the King James Version:

Isaiah 52:1-12	
King James Version	**International Standard Version**
Awake, awake; put on thy strength, O Zion; put on thy beautiful garments, O Jerusalem, the holy city: for henceforth there shall no more come into thee the uncircumcised and the unclean.	*Awake, awake! Clothe yourself with strength, O Zion! Put on your beautiful garments, O Jerusalem, the holy city, for the uncircumcised and the unclean won't enter you.*
Shake thyself from the dust; arise, and sit down, O Jerusalem: loose thyself from the bands of thy neck, O captive daughter of Zion.	*Shake yourself from the dust and arise, and sit on your throne, O Jerusalem! Loosen the bonds from your neck, O captive daughter of Zion.*
For thus saith the LORD, Ye have sold yourselves for nought; and ye shall be redeemed without money.	*For this is what the LORD says: "You were sold for nothing, and you'll be redeemed without money."*
For thus saith the Lord GOD, My people went down aforetime into Egypt to sojourn there; and the Assyrian oppressed them without cause.	*For this is what the LORD says: "My people went down long ago into Egypt to live there; the Assyrian, too, has oppressed them without cause.*

Now therefore, what have I here, saith the LORD, that my people is taken away for nought? they that rule over them make them to howl, saith the LORD; and my name continually every day is blasphemed.	*"Now therefore, what am I doing here," asks the LORD, "seeing that my people are taken away without cause? Those who rule over them are deluded," says the LORD, "and continuously, all the day long, my name is blasphemed.*
Therefore my people shall know my name: therefore they shall know in that day that I am he that doth speak: behold, it is I.	*Therefore my people will know my name; in that day they'll know that it is I who speaks, 'Here I am!'*
How beautiful upon the mountains are the feet of him that bringeth good tidings, that publisheth peace; that bringeth good tidings of good, that publisheth salvation; that saith unto Zion, Thy God reigneth!	*"How beautiful on the mountains are the feet of the one who brings news of peace, who announces good things, who announces salvation, who says to Zion, 'Your God reigns!'*

Thy watchmen shall lift up the voice; with the voice together shall they sing: for they shall see eye to eye, when the LORD shall bring again Zion.	Listen! Your watchmen lift up their voices, together they sing for joy; for they will see in plain sight the return of the LORD to Zion with compassion.
Break forth into joy, sing together, ye waste places of Jerusalem: for the LORD hath comforted his people, he hath redeemed Jerusalem.	"Break forth together into singing, you ruins of Jerusalem; for the LORD has comforted his people, and he has redeemed Jerusalem.
The LORD hath made bare his holy arm in the eyes of all the nations; and all the ends of the earth shall see the salvation of our God.	The LORD has bared his holy arm in the eyes of all the nations; and all the ends of the earth will see the salvation of our God.
Depart ye, depart ye, go ye out from thence, touch no unclean thing; go ye out of the midst of her; be ye clean, that bear the vessels of the LORD.	"Depart! Depart! Go out from there; touch no unclean thing; go out from the midst of her; purify yourselves, you who carry the vessels of the LORD.

For ye shall not go out with haste, nor go by flight: for the LORD will go before you; and the God of Israel will be your reward.	*For you won't go out in haste, nor will you go in flight; for the LORD will go before you; and the God of Israel will be your rear guard. He is called the God of all the earth."*

This is obviously Messianic. Here we see a sweeping portrayal of the Second Coming, with Jerusalem and the nation as its subject. It describes a time of rejoicing when the LORD returns to redeem Jerusalem, and all the earth will see God's salvation. The people have been oppressed, sold for nothing, but now the King is ready to say, "Here I am!"

Beginning in the next verse, however, we see a refocusing away from Zion and onto a specific individual: the Suffering Servant. Three verses from the end of chapter 52, Isaiah shifts from the nation to an individual:

Isaiah 52:13-15	
King James Version	**International Standard Version**
Behold, my servant shall deal prudently, he shall be exalted and extolled, and be very high.	*"Look! My servant will prosper, and he will be exalted and lifted up, and will be very high.*

As many were astonied at thee; his visage was so marred more than any man, and his form more than the sons of men:	*Just as many were astonished at you - so was he marred in his appearance, more than any human, and his form beyond that of human semblance -*
So shall he sprinkle many nations; the kings shall shut their mouths at him: for that which had not been told them shall they see; and that which they had not heard shall they consider.	*so will he startle many nations. Kings will shut their mouths at him; for what had not been told them they will see, and what they had not heard they will understand..."*

The Suffering Servant

There is a clear shift at this point in the book of Isaiah. The Messiah the King will appear and rule the world, but here we find that this same Servant will go through tremendous suffering. From verse 13 onward, we begin to see a portrait of Jesus Christ.

> *Behold, my servant shall deal prudently, he shall be exalted and extolled, and be very high.*

Isaiah 52:13

I am intrigued when I go to Israel and stand at Golgotha. There's a theory out there that the cross was not as tall as it's portrayed in our current media, but when we read John 3, we find that Jesus associates Himself with the brazen serpent in Numbers 21. Jesus tells Nicodemus in John 3:14-15, "*And as Moses lifted up the serpent in the wilderness, even so must the Son of man be lifted up: That whosoever believeth in him should not perish, but have eternal life*," which leads up to the most famous verse in the New Testament, John 3:16. The serpent was raised up so that all the Israelites could see it, and by looking on it they could be healed. I believe Jesus was raised very high on that cross. The Romans intended the cross to be an excruciating and slow form of execution, but it was also very public and visible. The victims were lifted high as a warning to other potential malefactors.

What was intended as a display of shame, however, has become the most praiseworthy and glorious act of self-sacrifice in the history of humankind. Jesus was raised up high, visible to those in Jerusalem, and from there His fame has reached to all the earth. All who look to Him for salvation will be healed, and one day the whole world will see Him and will worship Him.

The King James translators deliberately tone down verse 14, because the literal is difficult to handle. The ISV offers the more descriptive wording:

> *Just as many were astonished at you -*
> *so was he marred in his appearance,*

more than any human, and his form
beyond that of human semblance.

Isaiah 52:14

That's hard to imagine. The Roman soldiers abused and tortured Jesus with such severity that He couldn't be recognized as a human. Isaiah 50:6 gives us a detail that is often missed; they ripped off His beard. That might be one reason Mary Magdalene was slow to recognize Him on Sunday morning. John 20:15 says she initially mistook Him for the gardener. She wasn't expecting to find Jesus alive, and she was weeping, but if His face was beardless and scarred, He certainly didn't look like Himself.

So shall he sprinkle many nations; the
kings shall shut their mouths at him: for
that which had not been told them shall
they see; and that which they had not
heard shall they consider.

Isaiah 52:15

The word here for "sprinkle" is נזה - *nazah*. In the Law, the priests were often required to sprinkle sacrificial blood on things as a purification ritual. The other word translated "sprinkle" is *zaraq*. The sprinkling marks and covers things to make them holy, and it's done by one who is pure and innocent. There are some who argue that the term *nazah* always means to sprinkle something, a liquid or oil, and not to besprinkle a person or thing. They therefore translate it, "to scatter many nations," or "to surprise many nations." However, we find that that the term does mean to "besprinkle" in certain instances, as when Aaron is sprinkled (*nazah*) in Exodus 29:21. It's a priestly term, and its significance can be found in a study of the word *nazah* in the books of Moses.[13]

We find that "*the kings shall shut their mouths at him.*" This is a sign of respect. His very presence will cause the kings of the earth to stop speaking. It reminds us of Job 29:9: "*The princes refrained talking, and laid their hand on their mouth.*"

With this small teaser, we enter the next chapter.

Chapter 53

It's valuable to first read the entire passage before we consider each verse at a time. Again, I like to compare the KJV and the ISV side by side.

Isaiah 53:1-12	
King James Version	**International Standard Version**
Who hath believed our report? and to whom is the arm of the LORD revealed?	*Who has believed our message, and to whom has the arm of the LORD been revealed?*

For he shall grow up before him as a tender plant, and as a root out of a dry ground: he hath no form nor comeliness; and when we shall see him, there is no beauty that we should desire him.	*For he grew up before him like a tender plant, and like a root out of a dry ground; he had no form and he had no majesty that we should look at him, and there is no attractiveness that we should desire him.*
He is despised and rejected of men; a man of sorrows, and acquainted with grief: and we hid as it were our faces from him; he was despised, and we esteemed him not.	*"He was despised and rejected by others, and a man of sorrows, intimately familiar with suffering; and like one from whom people hide their faces; and we despised him and did not value him.*
Surely he hath borne our griefs, and carried our sorrows: yet we did esteem him stricken, smitten of God, and afflicted.	*"Surely he has borne our sufferings and carried our sorrows; yet we considered him stricken, and struck down by God, and afflicted.*
But he was wounded for our transgressions, he was bruised for our iniquities: the chastisement of our peace was upon him; and with his stripes we are healed.	*But he was wounded for our transgressions, and he was crushed for our iniquities, and the punishment that made us whole was upon him, and by his bruises we are healed.*

All we like sheep have gone astray; we have turned every one to his own way; and the LORD hath laid on him the iniquity of us all.	*All we like sheep have gone astray, we have turned, each of us, to his own way; and the LORD has laid on him the iniquity of us all.*
He was oppressed, and he was afflicted, yet he opened not his mouth: he is brought as a lamb to the slaughter, and as a sheep before her shearers is dumb, so he openeth not his mouth.	*He was oppressed and he was afflicted, yet he didn't open his mouth; like a lamb that is led to the slaughter, as a sheep that before its shearers is silent, so he did not open his mouth.*
He was taken from prison and from judgment: and who shall declare his generation? for he was cut off out of the land of the living: for the transgression of my people was he stricken.	*"From detention and judgment he was taken away - and who can even think about his descendants? For he was cut off from the land of the living, he was stricken for the transgression of my people.*
And he made his grave with the wicked, and with the rich in his death; because he had done no violence, neither was any deceit in his mouth.	*Then they made his grave with the wicked, and with rich people in his death, although he had committed no violence, nor was there any deceit in his mouth."*

	Exaltation of the Servant:
Yet it pleased the LORD to bruise him; he hath put him to grief: when thou shalt make his soul an offering for sin, he shall see his seed, he shall prolong his days, and the pleasure of the LORD shall prosper in his hand.	*"Yet the LORD was willing to crush him, and he made him suffer. Although you make his soul an offering for sin, he will see his offspring, and he will prolong his days, and the will of the LORD will triumph in his hand.*
He shall see of the travail of his soul, and shall be satisfied: by his knowledge shall my righteous servant justify many; for he shall bear their iniquities.	*Out of the suffering of his soul he will see light and find satisfaction. And through his knowledge his servant, the righteous one, will make many righteous, and he will bear their iniquities.*
Therefore will I divide him a portion with the great, and he shall divide the spoil with the strong; because he hath poured out his soul unto death: and he was numbered with the transgressors; and he bare the sin of many, and made intercession for the transgressors.	*Therefore I will allot him a portion with the great, and he will divide the spoils with the strong; because he poured out his life to death, and was numbered with the transgressors; yet he carried the sins of many, and made intercession for their transgressions."*

We find a reference to this passage by the confused Ethiopian treasurer in Acts 8:27-40. He asks Philip, *"...of whom speaketh the prophet this? of himself, or of some other man?"* Then Philip starts from this passage to teach the man about Jesus. In fact, Philip was brought supernaturally to meet with the Ethiopian, and as soon as he finishes, the Holy Spirit *"caught away Philip"* (v.39) and he disappears.

And so,

> *Who hath believed our report? and to*
> *whom is the arm of the LORD revealed?*
> Isaiah 53:1

John quotes this verse in John 12:38, as I mentioned in the last chapter. John continues in verse 41:

> *"These things said Esaias, when he saw*
> *his glory, and spake of him. Nevertheless*
> *among the chief rulers also many believed*
> *on him; but because of the Pharisees they*
> *did not confess him, lest they should be put*
> *out of the synagogue:"*

One of the interesting observations I've made from my own Bible studies is that many Pharisees and priests were, at least secretly, believers in Christ. We can't find any Sadducees who turned to Christ. The Pharisees were extremely conservative and legalistic, but they were dedicated to God and some saw their Messiah in Jesus Christ. The Sadducees, on the other hand, were the "moderns" of that day. They denied the existence of angels and the resurrection of the body, and I cannot find any place in the Scriptures where Sadducees were saved.

> *For he shall grow up before him as a tender plant, and as a root out of a dry ground: he hath no form nor comeliness; and when we shall see him, there is no beauty that we should desire him.*

Isaiah 53:2

I was surprised to discover there's an allusion to Jesus' childhood in Psalm 69:7-8. Psalm 69:8 tells us He became a stranger even to His own brothers, His mother's children. I believe Jesus came from an unhappy childhood, rejected by those around Him. As an adult, His own brothers failed to recognize His authority – until after the Resurrection.[14]

It's also interesting that Isaiah speaks of the Messiah as a root out of the dry ground. He is the root of Jesse, the father of David, as Isaiah 11 makes clear: "*And in that day there shall be a root of Jesse, which shall stand for an ensign of the people; to it shall the Gentiles seek: and his rest shall be glorious.*" We see this same label in Revelation 5:5, where He is called the "*Root of David.*"

We are used to thinking of a "root" as the source of something, and so it is. Yet, we have here a picture of new growth, a sprout out of a stump or trunk. Isaiah 11:1 states:

"And there shall come forth a rod out of the stem of Jesse, and a Branch shall grow out of his roots:" In Revelation 22:16, Jesus calls Himself the "root and offspring of David."

He is the offspring of David, sprouting out from dry ground. He is not entering the world in a friendly, comfortable manner. He was a tender plant, but He didn't attract love from the beginning. He wasn't desired.

He is despised and rejected of men; a man of sorrows, and acquainted with grief: and we hid as it were our faces from him; he was despised, and we esteemed him not.

Isaiah 53:3

Isaiah is describing this man, and he includes himself in the "we." He is referring to his own people Israel, but that "we" also includes us Gentiles. We all hid our faces from Him and we failed to esteem Him. We are all at fault. Christ was placed on that cross for each one of us – each of us nailed Him to that tree by our sins.

Matthew 27 highlights all of this for us. The Jews handed Jesus over to the Romans, and the Romans spit and beat on Jesus. They put the crown of thorns on Him and a robe and made fun of Him. After Jesus was crucified, the chief priests and elders mocked Him, and even one of the thieves crucified with Him threw His words in His face.

Today, the Son of God is still despised. Through Him was all the universe created, and eventually every knee will bow and every tongue confess that Jesus Christ is Lord, to the glory of God the Father.[15] Yet, even today Jesus is treated with contempt, and those who follow Him are despised as weak and foolish.

> *Surely he hath borne our griefs, and carried our sorrows: yet we did esteem him stricken, smitten of God, and afflicted.*
>
> Isaiah 53:4

The Gospels confirm that this passage was fulfilled in Jesus. In Matthew 8:17, the writer recognizes this Isaiah verse in Jesus' healing ministry: "*That it might be fulfilled which was spoken by Esaias the prophet, saying, Himself took our infirmities, and bare our sicknesses.*"

This is a strange picture of the Messiah that we find here in Isaiah 52 and 53. The Jews were expecting the Messiah to arrive in glory and victory. They were not ready for a despised, poor carpenter to come and pay for the sins of the nation. They expected a hero on a white horse; they were not ready for a baby placed in a manger. Yet, throughout the Old Testament the picture had been painted of the Lion who also came to serve as the sacrificial Lamb.

Chapter 3
Our Substitute

The 12 verses in Isaiah 53 essentially summarize all of Paul's epistles put together. It's important to notice as we proceed through this passage that the Suffering Servant purposely substituted Himself for us. His substitutionary character is not just declared but emphasized. He did not just die – He fulfilled specific details written centuries in advance. Substitution is the key throughout this passage. He suffered and died in our place.

> *But he was wounded for our transgressions, he was bruised for our iniquities: the chastisement of our peace was upon him; and with his stripes we are healed.*

Isaiah 53:5

Notice the repeated allusions to punishment exchange in this verse. It was for *our* transgressions that He was wounded. It was for *our* sins He was bruised. Every morning we should offer a prayer of thanksgiving as we try to understand what this means.

Jesus suffered at the end of His life, but don't forget that He sacrificed Himself just by coming to earth as a human. He was born of a woman so that we could be born of God. He humbled Himself so that we could be lifted up. He became a servant so that we could be made joint-heirs with Him. You and I can't imagine what that means. We are joint-heirs with Him? How can that even be possible? He is the God of the Universe, the King of Eternity. We are frail created beings. Yet, He suffered rejection so that we could become His friends. He denied Himself so that we could freely receive all things. He gave Himself so that He could bless us. We should long to appreciate the greatness and graciousness of this God we serve!

We Are Healed

"By His stripes we are healed." These words are often misunderstood, and I want to take a moment to address them. Many people take this verse and insist that the cross of Christ purchased physical and medical healing. That is, some people argue that we should never have any physical ailments. That's not exactly true. If it were, then the Apostle Paul didn't know it. God worked many miracles and healings through Paul,[16] yet he had to leave his friend Trophimus sick in Miletus.[17] In 1 Timothy 5:23, Paul gives Timothy advice concerning his frequent illnesses. God does have the power to heal us, and sometimes He does so. However, this verse in Isaiah refers to salvation and not medical healing. The cross has healed us from the spiritual effects of sin.

Our anchor for interpreting this verse is 1 Peter 2:24: "*Who his own self bare our sins in his own body on the tree, that we, being dead to sins, should live unto righteousness: by whose stripes ye were healed.*"

Peter does not focus on medical, physical healing but something vastly more profound. By Christ's stripes we are healed spiritually. I want to emphasize this, because it's easy to get caught in a trap. If Christ's beating and death on the cross guaranteed our medical healing, then how do we explain those situations when a believer is not healed – like Timothy or Trophimus or Paul himself? They were saved. They were faithful, beloved servants of Jesus Christ, and yet they were not healed in every situation. In 2 Corinthians 12:7-9 we find that Paul asked God three times to remove some mysterious thorn in the flesh, and God did not. Instead, the Lord said, "*My grace is sufficient for thee: for my strength is made perfect in weakness.*"

I've experienced some very serious losses in my own family, but I know that God loves me and He loves my family members. Miraculous physical healings do take place today. People are instantly healed of terrible diseases and cancers, blindness and addictions – name it. Yet, God's sovereignty is involved in every instance. Sometimes He heals people immediately, and sometimes He doesn't for His own reasons. Our eternal security does not hang on God's physical healing. Our salvation was purchased at the cross, and by Christ's stripes we are healed. Our security in Christ vastly overshadows every other issue.

Here is where our confidence lies:

My sheep hear my voice, and I know them, and they follow me: And I give unto them eternal life; and they shall never perish, neither shall any man pluck them out of my hand. My Father, which gave them me, is greater than all; and no man is able to pluck them out of my Father's hand.

John 10:27-29

We are safe in the palm of His hands. God's hands are big, and we are safe with Him.

All Things Work Together for Good

I have a tab in my Bible at Romans 8. Whenever there's a cloud on my horizon, I jump right into Romans 8 and check to make sure that verse 28 is still there. We cannot read Romans 8:28-39 and have any doubt about where we stand with respect to Christ.

And we know that all things work together for good to them that love God, to them who are the called according to his purpose.

Romans 8:28

Nay, in all these things we are more than conquerors through him that loved us. For I am persuaded, that neither death,

*nor life, nor angels, nor principalities, nor
powers, nor things present, nor things to
come, Nor height, nor depth, nor any other
creature, shall be able to separate us from
the love of God, which is in Christ Jesus
our Lord.*

Romans 8:37-39

Understanding and embracing these verses
are essential for our fruitfulness in the Lord's
ministry. If we harbor doubts about where we
stand with Christ, there's no way we can be
effective ambassadors for Him. We already spend
too much time worrying about our own failings
and focusing on the storms in our lives. We need to
focus on the faithfulness and love of God, rejoicing
in His goodness no matter what life throws at us.
Jesus never said that He would take away all our
problems. He said:

*These things I have spoken unto you, that
in me ye might have peace. In the world
ye shall have tribulation: but be of good
cheer; I have overcome the world.*

We need to nail this one down. Seriously.
Trusting in God's love – depending on God's love
and faithfulness – is essential for good spiritual
hygiene. We need to remember every day that
all things work together for good to those of us
who love God and are called for His purposes.
All things.

Remember that He gave Himself for us. Jesus Christ died in our place, taking our stripes on Himself. He loves us that much. That's why we can know with all confidence that He'll never drop us. We are far too valuable to Him to treat lightly. He never stops thinking about us. No matter what terrible storms of life face us, we can rest confident that He will make all things work for good for us.

Who Knew No Sin

All we like sheep have gone astray; we have turned every one to his own way; and the LORD hath laid on him the iniquity of us all.

Isaiah 53:6

The longer I live, the more I realize we have no idea what that involved.

Paul tells us in 2 Corinthians 5:21:

For he hath made him to be sin for us, who knew no sin; that we might be made the righteousness of God in him.

You and I can't imagine what that means. The holy, perfect Jesus, the Son of God was made sin on our behalf? We have no concept of that. It's a gap that we can't even imagine, yet it was bridged by God for our benefit. There on Calvary, Jesus became the brazen serpent raised up on a pole as He told Nicodemus in John 3:14.

Again, we find this declaration of substitutionary death. All our sin was laid on Him. That's unfathomable.

The Silent Lamb

*He was oppressed, and he was afflicted,
yet he opened not his mouth: he is brought
as a lamb to the slaughter, and as a sheep
before her shearers is dumb, so he openeth
not his mouth.*

Isaiah 53:7

We are like sheep gone astray, but He is a lamb brought to the slaughter. He is afflicted and has every right to complain, but He makes no noise. It's amazing to me, as I started digging into this, how Christ's silence is hammered away in all the four Gospels and Acts. Jesus stood there before His accusers while they attacked and condemned Him, and He said nothing.

Matthew tells us:

*And the high priest arose, and said unto
him, Answerest thou nothing? what is it
which these witness against thee? But Jesus
held his peace…"* [18]

Jesus didn't respond. His silence was so noticeable that the high priest called attention to it. In fact, Jesus' persistent silence draws out some passion in the high priest, and in Matthew 26:63 he demands, "*I adjure thee by the living God, that thou tell us whether thou be the Christ, the Son of God.*"

Only then does Jesus finally speak. The high priest thereby placed Jesus under oath, and the Law required that He respond, so He did. In the next verse:

> *Jesus saith unto him, Thou hast said: nevertheless I say unto you, Hereafter shall ye see the Son of man sitting on the right hand of power, and coming in the clouds of heaven.*

This is not a light statement. Jesus is quoting Daniel 7, in which the "Son of Man" is given all power:

> *I saw in the night visions, and, behold, one like the Son of man came with the clouds of heaven, and came to the Ancient of days, and they brought him near before him. And there was given him dominion, and glory, and a kingdom, that all people, nations, and languages, should serve him: his dominion is an everlasting dominion, which shall not pass away, and his kingdom that which shall not be destroyed.*
> Daniel 7:13-14

Here Jesus is at trial, being falsely accused, and He's bearing it in silence. When He is forced to say something, what does He tell the high priest? He says, "One day you'll see Me take over the world." I think every heart present should have been struck with fear.

It always amazes me when critics say that Christ never claimed to be God. They haven't read their Bibles closely enough. In John 8:58-59, the Jews wanted to stone Jesus because He stated, "*before Abraham was, I AM.*" In that statement, He claimed to be YHWH, the I AM, the voice in the Burning Bush. He claimed to have existed before Abraham. Anytime we miss Jesus' claims to be God, the Jews help us by wanting to stone Him. In John 10:30-33, Jesus said, "*I and My Father are one*" and they took up stones to stone Him.

The claim to be the I AM is massively significant. When the soldiers went to arrest Jesus in John 18:5-6, He said, "I am (Jesus of Nazareth)." As soon as He said, "I am," the officers fell backward. Jesus' simple statement, "I am," knocked the officers backwards. Jesus absolutely claimed to be God.

The high priest asks Jesus if He is the Christ, the Son of God. Under oath, Jesus responds in the affirmative, and then declares that He will come in the clouds in fulfillment of Daniel 7. The high priest doesn't leave us any room for confusion; he tears his robes and accuses Jesus of blasphemy.

Unless an answer was forced from Him, Jesus kept His peace. He also remained silent before Pilate later that morning:

And when he was accused of the chief priests and elders, he answered nothing. Then said Pilate unto him, Hearest thou not how many things they witness against thee? And he answered him to never a word; insomuch that the governor marvelled greatly.

Matthew 27:12-14

Jesus didn't say a word. As we study the trials of Jesus, we discover that Pilate, the personal representative of the ruler of the world, declared Him innocent seven different times.[19] Pilate tried every administrative trick he could think of to avoid putting Jesus to death.

When Pilate finds out Jesus is a Galilean, he realizes "Aha! I can lay this on Herod." So he gets Herod into the picture, and Herod hopes that Jesus will perform a miracle for him. However, while Jesus does break His silence for the high priest and for Pilate when He's pushed, He says absolutely nothing before Herod. Luke 23:9-11 tells us that Herod asks Him many questions but gets nothing, so he has his men mock Jesus and then sends Him back to Pilate.

Even though Jesus is innocent, He never worries about making a defense for Himself. When Pilate heard that He was the Son of God, he got shaken up, and he questions Jesus again in John 19:9: "*And went again into the judgment hall, and saith unto Jesus, Whence art thou? But Jesus gave him no answer.*"

Over and over the New Testament tells us Jesus remained silent on that fateful day. Jesus knows His purpose is to die, and He's just spent the night in emotional agony. The trial process is small potatoes compared to the job before Him.

This is the passage that the Ethiopian Treasurer was reading when the Spirit of God sent Philip to him. The Ethiopian went to Jerusalem to worship, and he's on his way home, puzzled. He has heard that the Messiah came, but He's been killed, so the Ethiopian is confused. The Lord sends Philip to tutor him and clear his understanding, and Philip starts with these verses in Isaiah.

> *He was taken from prison and from judgment: and who shall declare his generation? for he was cut off out of the land of the living: for the transgression of my people was he stricken.*
>
> Isaiah 53:8

It's absolutely astonishing to realize that this is the Creator Himself. He was crucified on a cross of wood, yet He made the hill on which it stood. It's astonishing to read about the crucifixion when we realize who is being crucified. At any time, Jesus could have said, "Enough already. I'm out of here." What held Him to that cross? It wasn't the nails.

It was His commitment to you and me – His love for you and me.

All four Gospels tell us that Pilate was impressed with Jesus and recognized His innocence. In all four accounts, we see that Pilate tried to get the Jews to take Jesus instead of Barabbas.[20]

I urge you to study the predicament of Barabbas. He was a robber and had been thrown into prison for murder and sedition. The Jewish leaders were so keen on executing Jesus that they were willing to let a murderer go free. It's important that we pay attention to the story of Barabbas because he provides a picture of our own situation. Here, the guilty and the innocent change places. The one that was guilty was declared innocent, and the One that was innocent was declared guilty. You and I are in the same shoes as Barabbas. We know we're guilty and Jesus is innocent – yet we've each changed places with Him. Our guilt was placed on Him.

My People

It's interesting that Isaiah states, "*for the transgression of my people was He stricken*." The common rabbinical Jewish interpretation of Isaiah 53 is that the "Suffering Servant" is the Jewish people – specifically the faithful Jewish remnant – persecuted by Gentiles. Verse 53:8 contradicts this view because Isaiah tells us the Suffering Servant dies *for* the sin of His people. Who were Isaiah's people? They were the inhabitants of Judah – the descendants of Israel.

Throughout Isaiah 52, God is proclaiming the redemption of Jerusalem and "My people" Israel, using Isaiah as His mouthpiece. While He is still speaking to Zion and His people, He begins to talk about His Servant. He speaks about the Servant as somebody different than "you" – that is, His people.

As Isaiah 53 opens, Isaiah keeps speaking about the Servant as a distinct individual. He repeatedly says "we" in opposition to the Servant:

> 53:3 ...*we* hid as it were *our* faces from *him*;
> he was despised, and *we* esteemed *him* not.
> 53:4 ...*he* hath borne *our* griefs, and carried
> *our* sorrows: yet *we* did esteem *him*
> stricken, smitten of God, and afflicted.
> 53:5 ...*he* was wounded for *our*
> transgressions, *he* was bruised for *our*
> iniquities: the chastisement of *our* peace
> was upon *him*; and with *his* stripes *we*
> are healed.
> 53:6 All *we* like sheep have gone astray
> … and the LORD hath laid on *him* the
> iniquity of us all.

We see throughout Isaiah 53 a pattern of "we" versus "him." The poor treatment of the Jews did not heal anybody. They bore no griefs and carried no sorrows but their own. They have not been silent like lambs before their shearers. Throughout Isaiah, even when God calls Israel His "servant," God is the One who comes as their Savior and

Redeemer.[21] The glory is never to Israel, but to God. All of us have gone astray. Only Jesus could take away the iniquity of us all.

Philip saw that this passage pointed directly to Jesus – not to the Israeli people. While reading this passage, the Ethiopian asks Philip whether Isaiah is talking about himself or another person, and Philip immediately starts from this verse to teach the Ethiopian about Jesus as the Messiah from the Hebrew Scriptures.

> *And he made his grave with the wicked,*
> *and with the rich in his death; because*
> *he had done no violence, neither was any*
> *deceit in his mouth.*

Isaiah 53:9

That's kind of strange. He made His grave with the wicked and yet He's with the rich. It doesn't say the "wicked rich" but "with the wicked *and* with the rich." That's interesting. It's interesting that Jesus' grave is in an area that's surrounded by other graves. In his commentary on Leviticus, Andrew Bonar builds a description of the tomb of Christ.[22] He explains that it was Levitically clean, being carved out of the rock. I've been to the Garden Tomb, and if you've been there, you can see Andrew Bonar's description in all its reality as he details the tomb of Christ. The shocker is that Andrew Bonar's commentary on Leviticus was published 40 years before General Gordon discovered what we now call the Garden Tomb.

That blew me away. From just the text of Leviticus, Andrew Bonar put together what we now take for granted.

The tour guides don't present the Garden Tomb as *the* tomb of Christ. They present it as representative, and it's to their credit they don't oversell it. However, I have spent a lot of time on this, and I happen to believe that the Garden Tomb is the actual tomb of Christ, based on 18 specifications. I might not be right, but it does fit every one of the descriptive requirements. It was clearly the tomb of one of the richest people in the area. It was among the graves of the wicked and yet with the rich. Jesus was a poor carpenter who had nothing, not even a place to rest His head,[23] yet He was buried in a rich man's grave. The Gospels consistently tell us that Joseph of Arimathaea had Jesus buried:

> *When the even was come, there came a rich man of Arimathaea, named Joseph, who also himself was Jesus' disciple: He went to Pilate, and begged the body of Jesus. Then Pilate commanded the body to be delivered. And when Joseph had taken the body, he wrapped it in a clean linen cloth, And laid it in his own new tomb, which he had hewn out in the rock: and he rolled a great stone to the door of the sepulchre, and departed.*

Matthew 27:57-60

The very fact that Joseph of Arimathea was able to go to Pilate and ask for Jesus' body tells us that the man had some clout. The average person wasn't free to pop in on the governor, the personal representative of the ruler of the world. Joseph clearly had influence and connections. The text tells us directly that Joseph was rich, and he was obviously the most connected and influential person among Jesus' disciples. He'd had a family sepulchre cut out of the rock, which separates the tomb Levitically from the graves of the wicked people who might be around it.

I like to imagine Pilate's asking Joseph of Arimathea, "What? You want to take your own tomb you've carved out for your family and give it to this criminal?" and hearing Joseph answer, "Oy vey, it's just for the weekend!"

Now, the Pharisees knew that Jesus had said He would rise again. The disciples were a little more thick-skulled, but it was clear to the Pharisees because they went to Pilate to ensure Jesus stayed dead.

> *Now the next day, that followed the day*
> *of the preparation, the chief priests and*
> *Pharisees came together unto Pilate,*
> *Saying, Sir, we remember that that*
> *deceiver said, while he was yet alive,*
> *After three days I will rise again.*
> *Command therefore that the sepulchre*

*be made sure until the third day, lest his
disciples come by night, and steal him
away, and say unto the people, He is risen
from the dead: so the last error shall be
worse than the first. Pilate said unto them,
Ye have a watch: go your way, make it as
sure as ye can. So they went, and made
the sepulchre sure, sealing the stone,
and setting a watch.*

Matthew 27:62-66

"*So the last error shall be worse than the first.*"
That's interesting. They admitted this whole thing
was a big mistake. See, they had not planned to
kill Jesus on a holiday. Jesus had forced their hand.
He controlled the timing when He announced at
the Last Supper that He was going to be betrayed
and sent Judas off to do what he had planned
to do.[24]

The Pharisees were afraid. They asked the
Roman authorities to make sure that no one
could steal the body of Jesus. The Romans had the
resources to put a very good guard on that tomb,
and I love how Pilate says, "make it as sure as you
can." I can hear Pilate's skepticism, and I don't
think he was surprised when he learned that the
tomb was empty three days later.

There are all kinds of legends about what
happened to Pilate after that, but none of them
have any real authority. The Coptics in Egypt have
a tradition that he became a believer, but none of

the traditions about him have any substantiation, so we don't know. Studying the text on that fateful day, though, I will not be surprised if I see Pilate when I get to Heaven. I have no doubt that Nebuchadnezzar is in Heaven, and it wouldn't surprise me to have Pilate there. It wouldn't surprise me at all.

Isaiah 53:9 finishes: "…*because he had done no violence, neither was any deceit in his mouth.*"

Once again, the final part of this verse applies to Jesus and not to Israel. The Hebrew Scriptures repeatedly rebuke Israel and Judah for lies and deceit, and they tell us God wrought salvation by His own arm.[25] Only Christ remained pure in both actions and words. In 1 Peter 2:22, Peter describes the humility of Christ:

> *Who did no sin, neither was guile found in his mouth: Who, when he was reviled, reviled not again; when he suffered, he threatened not; but committed himself to him that judgeth righteously:*

From the beginning of the world, God knew He would sacrifice His Son as a lamb for our wickedness.[26] John tells us in Revelation 13:8 that Jesus Christ is the, "Lamb slain from the foundation of the world." Satan had already sinned and led one-third of the angels to rebel with him. God knew Adam and Eve would sin and corrupt the entire human race. God purposed the sacrifice of His Son from the very beginning - to take on Himself the problem of sin and rebellion once-for-all.

> *Yet it pleased the LORD to bruise him;*
> *he hath put him to grief: when thou shalt*
> *make his soul an offering for sin, he shall*
> *see his seed, he shall prolong his days, and*
> *the pleasure of the LORD shall prosper in*
> *his hand.*
>
> Isaiah 53:10

It seems strange that it "pleased" the LORD to bruise His Son, but we know that Christ endured the cross, *"for the joy set before Him."* [27] God wasn't considering the pain; He was considering the joy of saving us. That's incredible to realize – He values us so greatly!

Paul tells us in Philippians 2:5-11 that Jesus willingly took the form of a servant and laid down His life, and God will exalt Him above all. One day every knee will bow and every tongue confess that Jesus Christ is Lord, *"to the glory of God the Father."*

> *He shall see of the travail of his soul, and*
> *shall be satisfied: by his knowledge shall my*
> *righteous servant justify many; for he shall*
> *bear their iniquities.*
>
> Isaiah 53:11

In Acts 13, Paul is preaching at Antioch in Pisidia. He points out something:

> *"Be it known unto you therefore, men and brethren, that through this man is preached unto you the forgiveness of sins: And by Him all that believe are justified from all things, from which ye could not be justified by the law of Moses…"*

Acts 13:38-39

Wow. The Jews had believed that by keeping the Law they could be saved. If they followed all the commandments and applied the sacrificial system, they believed they were good with God. Yet, Paul points out the very real problem that the Law of Moses didn't actually justify anybody. For us to be justified, Christ had to come and die for the forgiveness of our sins, in fulfillment of Isaiah 53.

Paul continues this theme in Romans 5:18, saying, "*Therefore as by the offence of one judgment came upon all men to condemnation; even so by the righteousness of one the free gift came upon all men unto justification of life.*"

After all the effort and careful work the Jews had done in keeping the Law, it turns out that justification is a free gift. That's incredible.

The most amazing part of all is that He will bear the sins of many and make intercession for the transgressors. He took their sins and was still able to intercede for them? That's fantastic! Yet, that is exactly what we see in Jesus. After the terrible trauma of the day, hanging there on the cross dying, Jesus sought the pardon of the very men who had murdered Him.

> *Then said Jesus, Father, forgive them; for they know not what they do.*
>
> Luke 23:34

> *Therefore will I divide him a portion with the great, and he shall divide the spoil with the strong; because he hath poured out his soul unto death: and he was numbered with the transgressors; and he bare the sin of many, and made intercession for the transgressors.*
>
> Isaiah 53:12

This is staggering when we think about it. Jesus poured out His soul unto death. In verse eight we learned that He was cut off from the land of the living, and in verse nine we learned He made His grave with the rich and wicked. Yet, here we find God will give Him portions with the great and the strong.

This is the message of the New Testament, that Jesus Christ died to bear our sins and now sits at the right hand of the Father making intercession for us. Although He was innocent, He was treated as a criminal and killed as a criminal. He became sin for us so that we could be set free from sin, and because of His great love and mercy, God has made us joint-heirs with Him.

> *For there is one God, and one mediator between God and men, the man Christ Jesus; Who gave himself a ransom for all, to be testified in due time.*
>
> 1 Timothy 2:5-6

> *And if children, then heirs; heirs of God, and joint-heirs with Christ; if so be that we suffer with him, that we may be also glorified together.*
>
> Romans 8:17

> *Who is he that condemneth? It is Christ that died, yea rather, that is risen again, who is even at the right hand of God, who also maketh intercession for us.*
>
> Romans 8:34

> *Wherefore he is able also to save them to the uttermost that come unto God by him, seeing he ever liveth to make intercession for them. For such an high priest became us, who is holy, harmless, undefiled, separate from sinners, and made higher than the heavens;*
>
> Hebrews 7:25-26

Chapter 4
The God Outside of Time

Being justified freely by his grace through the redemption that is in Christ Jesus: Whom God hath set forth to be a propitiation through faith in his blood, to declare his righteousness for the remission of sins that are past, through the forbearance of God;

Romans 3:24-25

The word "propitiation" is a ten-dollar word in both English and Greek. In the Greek, it's *hilasmos* or *hilasterion*, which means "appeasement" or "atonement." This is the term for the mercy seat that was used to cover of the Ark of the Covenant. In the Holy of Holies, the mercy seat was sprinkled with the blood of a goat on *Yom Kippur* – the Day of Atonement – symbolizing the recompense for sins. Ultimately, the blood of the sacrificial animal symbolized the covering of the people by the blood of Christ, which Hebrews 10 explains in detail. *Yom Kippur* was made as a "*shadow of good things to come*"[28] – a ritual that anticipated the acting out of Christ's ultimate sacrifice on the cross.

Isaiah 53 is part of a message that threads throughout the Bible. That thread starts at the beginning in Genesis 3:15, when God declares war on Satan and announces that the *"seed of the woman"* would crush Satan's head. It continues from there to 2 Samuel 7:12 and 16, when God tells David:

> *…I will set up thy seed after thee, which shall proceed out of thy bowels, and I will establish his kingdom… and thine house and thy kingdom shall be established for ever before thee: thy throne shall be established for ever.*

In Psalm 2, we learn that God is going to war against His Son's enemies on the earth. Psalm 2 is a remarkable discussion among the three members of the Trinity: Father, Son and Holy Ghost.

The first 18 verses of Psalm 22 read as if they were declared by Christ as He hung on the cross. The virgin birth is announced in Isaiah 7, and we read Isaiah 9:6 on many of our Christmas cards:

> *For unto us a child is born, unto us a son is given: and the government shall be upon his shoulder: and his name shall be called Wonderful, Counsellor, The mighty God, The everlasting Father, The Prince of Peace.*

Isaiah 9:6

Isaiah 11 describes the Millennium, when Christ reigns on the earth.

Isaiah 53 describes the Messiah's purpose as the Suffering Servant who gives His life to die for sins in our place.

The first two verses of Isaiah 61 were Jesus' mandate in His first advent. When Jesus reads this passage in Luke 4:18-19, He stops at the comma and doesn't complete Isaiah 61:2. In His first visit, He was there to proclaim the "acceptable year of the LORD". The "vengeance" of our God comes later.

In Micah 5:2 we are told that the Messiah will be born in Bethlehem. We also learn something else very important about the One who will be ruler in Israel – that His *"goings forth have been from of old, from everlasting."* We often read lightly over verses like this without realizing their incredible significance.

In Zechariah 9:9, we learn that the Messiah will ride to Zion on a donkey, humble and just, bringing with Him salvation. Matthew 21, Mark 11, Luke 19 and John 12 all describe the entry of Jesus into Jerusalem, and we celebrate this joyous day every Palm Sunday. This is the one time, by the way, and the only time in the Gospels that Jesus presents Himself as a King to Jerusalem. It's a key day.

In Zechariah 11:12-13 we find that He is sold for 30 pieces of silver, which are thrown to the potter.[29]

There are a multitude of verses and types in the Old Testament that are fulfilled in Jesus Christ. I encourage you to make your own list and develop your own study. Track the First Coming of Jesus Christ prophesied throughout the Old Testament. We are still waiting for the Second Coming, and every day it draws closer. I sincerely believe that we are being plunged into a period of time about which the Bible says more than it does about any other period of time in all of history, including the time that Jesus walked the shores of Galilee and climbed the mountains of Judea.

Our God tells the end from the beginning, and before things come to pass He makes them known. He is a God outside of Time.

The Suffering Servant and Israel

Let's return to the first verse of Isaiah 53:

Who hath believed our report? and to whom is the arm of the LORD revealed?

Almost everyone who studies Isaiah 53 recognizes it as a piece of prophecy. It may come as a shock to realize that Isaiah 53 hasn't actually happened yet. What? Technically, this passage has not been fulfilled yet – not completely.

Why?

Because it is recording: "*To whom is the arm of the Lord revealed?*" That is, it is recording Israel's rejection of the Messiah and their subsequent discovery of Him. Initially, the people of Israel turn away from the Messiah and reject Him, but later they embrace Him. What we read in these verses technically applies to that lifting of the fog – when the nation of Israel realizes that Jesus has indeed been the Messiah all this time. That hasn't happened yet.

Is the revelation coming to them? Yes, and that's when the world will be changed.

An Integrated Message

Epistemology is the study of knowledge, its scope and limits. What is our epistemological approach to this subject here? The first thing we do is establish the integrity of the Bible's design. We recognize that the Bible has integrity as a single story: we have 66 books penned by over 40 authors over thousands of years, and yet we find that it is an integrated message system, and it must clearly originate outside our time domain.

The God of the Bible is the God from outside of Time. He declares this in Isaiah:

> *Thus saith the LORD the King of Israel, and his redeemer the LORD of hosts; I am the first, and I am the last; and beside me there is no God.*

> Isaiah 44:6

> *I have declared the former things from the beginning; and they went forth out of my mouth, and I shewed them; I did them suddenly, and they came to pass…I have*

even from the beginning declared it to thee;
before it came to pass I shewed it thee…:

Isaiah 48:3, 5a

My technical specialty is Information Sciences. I have studied the design of the Bible's 66 books for many decades – the use of types and idioms, prophecy and fulfillment. From the deception of Eve by the serpent in Genesis though to Satan's final punishment in Revelation, it's clear that the Bible had to have been designed by a single Author. That's something we can each continue to study for the rest of our lives. Details that at first glance seem petty end up being incredibly important. As Paul told Timothy, "*All scripture is given by inspiration of God, and is profitable for doctrine, for reproof, for correction, for instruction in righteousness.*"[30]

These 66 separate books were written by 40 different guys who didn't even know each other, yet every detail is there by deliberate design, and it comes from outside the dimensionality of time. Thanks to Einstein we know that time is a physical property. God is not somebody "with a lot of time". He's outside of time altogether.

The Scriptures came to us by the Holy Spirit. Peter reminds us in 2 Peter 1:21, "*For the prophecy came not in old time by the will of man: but holy men of God spake as they were moved by the Holy Ghost.*" The Holy Spirit testifies about Jesus,[31] and the Holy Spirit inspired the Scriptures, so it follows that the Scriptures are filled with testimony about Jesus Christ. Jesus told the Jews in John 5:39,

"Search the scriptures; for in them ye think ye have eternal life: and they are they which testify of me."

As we establish the integrity of the design, we discover that Jesus is on every page. He's not just in the New Testament; He is throughout the whole package. What's more, the fact that Jesus is on every page of the Bible establishes who Jesus Christ is.

What does the Old Testament say about the Messiah? It says He would be:

- Of the line of David (2 Sam 7:12-16; Ps 89:3-4; 110:1; 132:11; Isa 9:6, 7; 11:1)
- Born of a virgin (Gen 3:15; Isa 7:14)
- Born in Bethlehem (Micah 5:2)
- A sojourner in Egypt (Hos 11:1)
- A Galilean (Isa 9:1, 2) and in Nazareth (Isa 11:1)[32]
- Announced by an Elijah-like herald (Isa 40:3-5; Mal 3:1; 4:5)
- An occasion for the slaughter of Bethlehem's children (Gen 35:19-20; Jer 31:15)
- Bringing liberty to the captives (Isa 58:6; 61:1)
- A hero to the Gentiles (Isa 42:1-4)
- A substitute for our griefs and punishment (Isa 53:4-5)
- A healer (Isa 53:4-5)
- A teacher of parables (Isa 6:9-10; Ps 78:2)
- Disbelieved, rejected (Ps 69:4; 118:22; Isa 6:10; 29:13; 53:1)

- A humble King entering Jerusalem (Zech 9:9; Ps 118:26)
- Betrayed by friend (Ps 41:9)
- Betrayed for 30 pieces of silver (Zech 11:1-13)
- Like a smitten shepherd (Zech 13:7)
- Given vinegar and gall (Ps 69:21)
- Pierced (Zech 12:10; Ps 22:16)
- Unbroken (like the Passover lamb) (Ex 12:46; Num 9:12; Ps 34:20)
- Killed along with malefactors (Isa 53:9, 12)
- Buried in a rich man's grave (Isa 53:9)
- Raised from the dead on the 3rd day (Gen 22:4; Ps 16:10-11; Jonah 1:7; Hos 6:2)
- Resurrected, followed by destruction of Jerusalem (Dan 9:26; 11:31; 12:1,11)

There are hundreds upon hundreds of prophetic types that Jesus fulfills.

When developing my epistemology, I take a multi-pronged approach. First, it's important to establish the integrity of the Bible's design. The next step is to recognize that the Bible describes the identity of this person called Jesus Christ. The final step is to understand that while Jesus was on Earth, He authenticated the rest of the package. That's my epistemological approach.

This world is filled with people who doubt God. If they don't doubt His existence, they doubt His nature and character. They doubt His love.

They doubt His ability and desire to communicate to us and move in our lives. The world is filled with skeptics who will challenge those with faith. It's vital that we know *why* we believe that Jesus is the Son of God – that we can defend our faith, and do so with the Spirit and love of God. The world needs to know that Jesus Christ really did die for us, and He really will return. What practical things can we do to help those around us – especially the hardened skeptics? God is not willing that any should perish [33]

Chapter 5
Answering the Skeptics

Entropy and Information

Many of us who have a background in physics and information sciences suspect that entropy – randomness that leads toward disorder – was introduced in Genesis 3 as part of God's curse. William Graham MacDonald has produced an idiomatic translation of the New Testament,[34] and in his version of Romans 8:20, Paul says, "*The creation was subjected to entropy, not by consent, but on account of the one who subjected it so as to involve hope.*" The created world is breaking down, and the entire creation is the subject of God's curse, not just mankind. Since the created world is also under the curse, the entire creation is therefore the beneficiary of what occurred on that cross erected in Judea over 2000 years ago.

In the next verse (in the King James) Paul says:

Because the creature itself also shall be delivered from the bondage of corruption into the glorious liberty of the children of God. For we know that the whole creation groaneth and travaileth in pain together until now.

You see what Paul is saying? He's emphasizing that the completed work of Jesus Christ involves the creation itself, breaking the curse that started in Genesis 3. This is the climax.

Entropy. The King James calls it, "the bondage of corruption." In the science of thermodynamics, no system operates in perfect efficiency; it always loses energy in the form of heat radiating into the universe. All things ultimately tend toward randomness. It takes more energy to maintain order than to fall out of order.

Faith in nature's magical ability to overcome entropy is undermining our entire culture. As a whole, the created world is tending toward disorder. That's what we observe. It contradicts the 2nd Law of Thermodynamics to argue that increased order happens by chance – that organisms engineer themselves over time. Statistically - mathematically - disorder always prevails. The House ultimately wins in Las Vegas. Entropy always wins in the game of order versus disorder.

Biologists operate under the misconception that their field is a lawbreaker in the universe - that somehow the laws of physics are suspended when it comes to biology, and in their field randomness creates more order than disorder.

Yet, entropy is the absence of an ordering force. To attribute design *to* randomness demonstrates ignorance. Those two words "design" and "randomness" are antithetical to each other. That's fundamental. It is the epitome of absurdity to ascribe the most elegant designs to random processes.

We see it in our cars. As soon as a $75,000 Jaguar leaves the lot, it loses value. By the time it has 100,000 miles on it, it can be purchased on Craigslist for one-tenth the price. Why? Because the various components begin wearing out, breaking down, and falling apart. Even the brilliant and effective DNA programming of our bodies is inefficient. Our biochemical processes generate wonderful amounts of heat that keep us warm, but we lose that energy to the air, and year after year random errors weaken our biological machinery. Our DNA-programmed processes slow and fail until we finally die.

Yet, we let the schools teach our children that they are the results of random processes – that the digital program of DNA somehow wrote and ordered itself over time.

What do we actually observe? We see that the DNA that *already* exists is breaking down. We see that errors creep in over time. Not every mutation causes harm; some mutations are useful in certain environments, some mutations are neutral, some are dangerous, and some are deadly. However, all mutations have one thing in common; not one creates new function. If they create a change, it is always caused by a breakdown in some function that once existed. For instance, white people cannot produce as much melanin as their darker brothers and sisters. That can be a problem in India where the sun burns hot, and it can be handy in Iceland, where there is little sun to generate vitamin D in our skin. However, the fact remains that we pale folks have lost much of mankind's ability to make melanin. We didn't gain anything *new* that gave us more light sensitivity at higher latitudes. Instead, we lost something that previously existed.

By definition, information is designated as negative entropy. Anytime we see design, a negative-entropy force was at work. Yet, we continue to teach our children that they are cosmic accidents, and we wonder why they have no sense of destiny.

The Ultimate Drama

Our real focus here is the divine conflict. We know that Satan fell and took a host of angels with him. From Revelation 12, we infer that a third of the angels followed in Satan's rebellion. As we read the Bible, we find a drama where Satan constantly works to thwart or confuse God's plan. Yet, time and again, God has the victory and makes Satan look foolish.

The amazing thing about the war declared in Genesis 3 is the central role we humans take. We find in Deuteronomy 4:32 where God says:

> *For ask now of the days that are past,*
> *which were before thee, since the day that*
> *God created man upon the earth, and ask*

from the one side of heaven unto the other,
whether there hath been any such thing as
this great thing is, or hath been heard
like it?

Deuteronomy 4:32

We are living in the greatest drama of all time, and it is unique to humans and the Earth. There is nothing else like it in all the universe. No greater story has ever been told or can ever be told, and our planet is the theater.

Science is supposed to be all about observation. Scientists gather data and make hypotheses based on their initial observations. They then test those hypotheses and gather more data until they are able to develop a theory, which they continue to test over and over again. That's the idea.

Yet, there are groups of scientists who hunt the world for the unobservable. Among these are astrobiologists, those who study life on other planets. Astronomers are able to indirectly perceive the presence of exoplanets, those circling other stars, but it's a tricky business. Those planets are detected by the tiny effects they have on their star, and determining the actual characteristics of candidate planets involves a lot of guesswork. Finding life? Currently impossible. Astrobiologists cannot actually access any planets outside our solar system, which makes astrobiology less than a real science. There's no way to test whether or not life exists out there.

Deuteronomy 4:32 calls its readers to, *"ask from one side of heaven unto the other"* whether anything had been ever done as God had done in Israel. The entire creation can be petitioned for an answer, but what does that entail? We know there is a heavenly host of angels and other spiritual beings; Job 38:7 tells us they shouted for joy when God created the earth. We can also ask, "Is there life in outer space?" If so, is it sinless or sinful? Jesus died once – and He did it here on this planet in our corner of the Milky Way Galaxy. All of creation became corrupted by the Fall. This universe will be rolled up like a scroll,[35] to be replaced by a new heavens and earth that will last forever.[36]

John tells us in his first chapter that all things were made through and by Jesus. Jesus was in the Beginning. The Creator of the world became flesh and dwelt among us – and that is the most compelling argument for the uniqueness of terrestrial life on the planet Earth. The Creator who made it all chose to take the form of a human child. He entered His own creation and when He died and rose again, He did so once and for all.[37] He did it here. The vastness of the universe only speaks to His immensity and power; it doesn't necessitate life on any other planet.

It's also important to understand that Jesus did not become a man for a mere 33 1/2 years. We discover the astonishing fact that there is *a human* sitting on the throne of God.

> *But this man, after he had offered one sacrifice for sins for ever, sat down on the right hand of God;*
>
> Hebrews 10:12

That's staggering; Jesus became a man for all eternity. We can spend the rest of our lives considering the implications of that fact.

There's nothing but bad news for the astrobiologists because they shouldn't confuse wishful thinking with evidence. Science is the study of evidence, and it depends on testability and repeatability. Astrobiologists have no evidence to study. They can discern possible perturbations around distant stars and argue that those perturbations might indicate the presence of planets – that's it. Despite extensive searching, there isn't any evidence of life beyond our own planet. There's speculations about water and atmosphere on those possible planets, but there's no biology to study. "Astrobiology" is a misnomer.

The belief that life can spontaneously evolve – here or somewhere else – is not science. It's religion. Science has become a priesthood, and those who do not adhere to the popular credos jeopardize their careers and reputations.

The incarnation of Jesus Christ is the crowning achievement of eternity. He's a universal Savior – not just for the Jews, but for every one of us. His death and resurrection are the mechanisms that God used to accomplish His purposes, and the covenant is unique to Earth, exclusive to humans, and universally unprecedented.

The Anthropic Principle

Even secular scientists have long recognized that Earth and the universe – the very laws and ratios that we find in nature – seem "just right" for life to exist. It's as though nature is perfectly balanced for our presence. The idea that the numbers we find in nature seem designed for the benefit of human life is called the Anthropic Principle. Scientists have cataloged more than 140 quantifiable characteristics that must fall within an extremely narrow window in order for physical life to exist – and not just life in general, but human life. If certain ratios in the universe were changed by even 1 in a million, life would be impossible. For instance, the fine structure constant *alpha* has a value of almost exactly 1/137. This "coupling constant" defines the strength of the electromagnetic force between electrically charged elementary particles like electrons and protons. Regarding the fine structure constant, physicist John Barrow of Cambridge states:

> *If we change it by a very small amount, say in the second decimal place, then the changes become more significant. Properties of atoms are altered and complicated processes like protein folding or DNA replication may be adversely affected...* [38]

If *alpha* were even a little bit weaker than that, elements like iron and copper and even carbon could not form, eliminating the existence of planets, let alone carbon-based life. Barrow and fellow physicist Frank Tipler wrote a book together called *The Anthropic Cosmological Principle* in which they go into detail about the many aspects of our universe that seem finely tuned for life.[39]

Barrow makes the argument that we only recognize the Anthropic Principle because we are here to recognize it. In any of a zillion other potential universes, we would not exist – but because we live in this one, we are able to comment about the amazingly large number of coincidences that have allowed our existence.

The problem with this argument is that we don't know whether any other universes exist. We do know *this* one exists, and we recognize that those multitude of convenient coincidences – all carefully balanced – can be statistically considered a miracle. All life on the earth came from the same source. All life on the earth is tied to that same source and is unique in the universe.

The pivotal passage in Isaiah 53 describes the astonishing personal sacrifice of the Creator Himself, which changes everything for us. Without it, we would have no hope; we'd be destined for eternal punishment. Because of that sacrifice, we have the opportunity to live with our Creator and King forever. It's the passage that gives us understanding of who our God is – and how

He operates! He's the sort of God that would give everything for us. That's who He is. That is why it's the fulcrum, the pivot of the entire drama.

The Great Delusion

As we step closer and closer to the Second Coming of Christ, we recognize a gigantic delusion is on the horizon. Satan knows that his time is short:

> *Therefore rejoice, ye heavens, and ye that dwell in them. Woe to the inhabiters of the earth and of the sea! for the devil is come down unto you, having great wrath, because he knoweth that he hath but a short time.*

Revelation 12:12

> *And I beheld another beast coming up out of the earth; and he had two horns like a lamb, and he spake as a dragon. And he exerciseth all the power of the first beast before him, and causeth the earth and them which dwell therein to worship the first beast, whose deadly wound was healed. And he doeth great wonders, so that he maketh fire come down from heaven on the earth in the sight of men, And deceiveth them that dwell on the earth by the means of those miracles which he had power to do in the sight of the beast; saying to them that dwell on the*

> *earth, that they should make an image*
> *to the beast, which had the wound by a*
> *sword, and did live.*

Revelation 13:11-14

The final deception is a subject for another study, but even now deceptive ideas parade through our culture. The best way to recognize a lie is to already know the truth. It's therefore vital that we know what the Bible says. It's vital that we know why we believe Jesus Christ is the Son of God and can trust the Bible as God's Word.

Isaiah 53 describes a time when the nation Israel discovers that the Suffering Servant was their Messiah all along. We see Satan's great deception on the horizon, but we also see that all Israel will know the Christ, even as Paul anticipates in Romans 11. That's yet to happen, but it is coming – and according to Hosea 5, it's the prerequisite to the Second Coming.

> *For I would not, brethren, that ye*
> *should be ignorant of this mystery, lest ye*
> *should be wise in your own conceits; that*
> *blindness in part is happened to Israel,*
> *until the fulness of the Gentiles be come*
> *in. And so all Israel shall be saved: as it is*
> *written, There shall come out of Sion the*
> *Deliverer, and shall turn away ungodliness*
> *from Jacob: For this is my covenant unto*
> *them, when I shall take away their sins.*

Romans 11:25-27

I will go and return to my place, till they acknowledge their offence, and seek my face: in their affliction they will seek me early.

Hosea 5:15

Chapter 6
Hidden Treasures

There's something very strange about the following paragraph. Can you identify it?

So this small town of Branton Hills was lazily snoozing amidst up-and-doing towns, as Youth's Champion, John Gadsby, took hold of it; and shook its dawdling, flabby body until its inhabitants thought a tornado had struck it. Call it tornado, volcano, military onslaught, or what you will, this town found that it had a bunch of kids who had wills that would admit of no snoozing; for that is Youth, on its forward march of inquiry, thought and action.[43]

The odd thing about this little paragraph is what it's *missing*. The author, Ernest Vincent Wright, wrote the entire 50,000-word story *Gadsby* in 1939 without once using the letter "e." In fact, Wright says he tied down the "e" on his typewriter so the letter couldn't slip in accidentally. He did it just to show that it could be done. It wasn't easy. The letter "e" is by far the most common in the English language, and Wright took great care to exclude "e" from every single word. He even avoided abbreviations like "Mr." and "Mrs." which are shortened forms of words that contain the letter "e" because we'd hear the "e" spoken if they were read out loud.

Difficult as it was, Wright merely removed one letter. Look at the Bible. We should have long suspected that the very letters in the Bible were placed with the greatest of care. In Matthew 5:18, Jesus declared, *"For verily I say unto you, Till heaven and earth pass, one jot or one tittle shall in no wise pass from the law, till all be fulfilled."*

I always get fascinated by some of these quaint perceptions that the rabbis have. We can learn a lot from them. The rabbis say when the Messiah comes, He will not only interpret the words and the letters, He'll even interpret the spaces between the letters. When I first heard that, I discarded it as a colorful exaggeration. I now suspect the rabbis are *more* correct than we could have ever known before the computer age.

A jot is the smallest of the 22 letters of the Hebrew alphabet, and it looks a lot like an apostrophe. A tittle is the little decorative hook on some of the Hebrew letters, something we might easily mistake for an apostrophe or a little blemish on the paper. If the very crossing of a "t" or the dotting of an "i" was important, then we should be taking a much closer look at the Scriptures than we allow by casual reading.

Jesus' point is that we need to take the text seriously. People who build their theologies on fanciful twisting of the text are playing with fire, because Jesus let us know that every jot and tittle matters. I will even argue that there are no synonyms. Two words may mean almost the same thing, but we need to be careful during Bible studies to develop a respect for the precision of words. With the software that's now available, people can study the Bible in Hebrew and Greek without even knowing those languages. There are wonderful exegetical, expositional resources available for free on the Internet, and libraries in even the smallest towns have computers available for research. There's very little excuse not to do our homework.

The very letters of the Bible are important, and we've grown to appreciate the significance of this in the 20th century more than ever before. The computer age has given us many things, including the ability to crunch through the letters of the Bible and find codes hidden there for millennia.

Hebrew and Cryptography

The study of secret writing, cryptography, has many techniques derived from the ancient Hebrew sages. Hebrew has a strange alphabet. It is shorter than the English alphabet with 22 letters rather than 26, and Hebrew has no vowels. Vowels tend to be redundant, and it's important to avoid redundancy in the encryption of secret messages. One of the first things to do when making an encryption is to toss out the vowels and put them back in later. Hebrew has no vowels to begin with, making it convenient for encryption.

Hebrew is unique in that it's not just phonetic, it's sememic. That is, each letter carries meaning. We are accustomed to alphabets where the combination of letters tells us how to pronounce the word. Those letters and groups of letters are phonemes. We read them according to how they sound, and the words they form give us meaning. Hebrew is phonetic, but it is also sememic. It's symbolic. Individual letters can have their own meanings.

Early in Hebrew writing, the letters were also pictographs. *Aleph*, for instance, was shaped like the head of an ox and represented strength and leadership. The letter *kaf* was originally shaped like a hand, and the word "*kaf*" means "palm of the hand" or "to coerce." In fact, the Hebrew Department at the University of Arizona pointed out to me that if they teach the students how to recognize Hebrew in terms of the ancient letters, it takes half an hour to learn the meaning of a large number of words. Hebrew words are based on three-letter base words, and by determining the meaning of the letters within the base word, one can get a feel for the meaning of the word itself. The students make a list of 22 Hebrew letters and learn them and what they signify. Once they do that, they can unravel up to 80% of Hebrew by making informed guesses about the semantics of the words in a passage.

Early Hebrew was much different than the Hebrew we see today. While the Jews were exiled in Babylon, they began using the letter forms of the Babylonians. The square script was easier to write, and the paleo-Hebrew used by Moses and David was largely abandoned. We know quite a bit about paleo-Hebrew because we still find it in ancient manuscripts and inscriptions. The Dead Sea Scrolls, for instance, include books of Moses written in the paleo-Hebrew script. The Mesha Stele in the Louvre Museum parallels 2 Kings 3:4-8 from the Moabite point of view. In the letters of paleo-Hebrew (although the Moabite language) it references Yahweh and Israel, including the "House of Omri" and the "House of David."

If the letters *aleph* and *bet* are written out in their original paleo-Hebrew form, they create an interesting illustration. The *aleph* shows the head of an ox and represents strength. The letter *bet* looks something like a house, and the word *bet* means "house." Bethlehem means "house of bread" and Bethel means "house of God." If we place an *aleph* and a *bet* together as the word אב - *ab* - in the ancient Hebrew, we get the word "father." We know this word – we know the word "*abba*" is "daddy" in Hebrew. What is the father? He is the strength of the house. See how that works?

Let's go one step further. The Hebrew letter ה - *heh* - is like a breath, and it may represent an open window that lets the breeze in. The letter implies a wind or spirit. Placing a *heh* in the middle of a word inserts a breath into that word. The word *aleph-heh-bet* - אהב - is therefore *aleph* and *bet* combined with a breath of life. The *heh* gives us the essence of the father. What is the essence of the father? It's the Hebrew word for love - אהב. Love is the essence of the father. In Genesis 17, when God changed the name of Abram to Abraham and Sarai to Sarah, God added a *heh* to their names, signifying the presence of the Spirit of God.

When we write, we place spaces between the words to separate them and avoid confusion. In ancient Greek and Latin and Hebrew, the letters were strung together without spaces. Hebrew has five letters that have a different form if they are the last letter in a word. The equivalents of our k, m, n, p, and t have final forms that indicate the end of the word, making the language self-parsing. What's more, each letter is given a numerical value, and the final form letters have different values than their more mundane versions. For instance, the letter *mem* has a numerical value of 40, but the final form *mem* has a value of 600.

Because of these things, Hebrew lends itself to wordplay – to acrostics and puns, transpositions, and even mysticism. We discover that the numerical value of the words can have relevance.

For instance, the numbers for the word "year" add up to 355, which is a lunar year of 12 months. So that leads to a sense of mysticism that gets exploited by some.

The natural result of all this is that ancient Hebrew sages developed what we think of today as cryptography – the writing of secret codes. A modern form of cryptography came into use during the Renaissance, since success at war and peace depended on being able to communicate secretly. The field of cryptography developed during warfare, especially in World War II, but the Hebrew sages had cornered the market on cryptography long before Germany produced its Enigma encryption machine.

The ELS Codes

At the age of 13, Rabbi Michael Ber Weissmandl acquired a commentary by a 13th century sage named Rabbenu Bachya ben Asher of Saragossa, in Spain. Young Weissmandl was fascinated by the notes made by this ancient Hebrew sage, because the rabbi kept making cryptic notes about the importance of skipping certain letters. That intrigued Weissmandl. He took the 304,805 letters of the Torah and wrote them out on 10 by 10 cards. For the rest of his life, Weissmandl maintained his certainty that divinely ordered information was embedded within the Torah. By writing out the letters in a grid, he was able to facilitate the identification of skipped-letter sequences. Thus, he rediscovered what we today call equidistant letter sequences (ELS).

It happens that ELS codes are not a very sophisticated form of encryption. It's not good at hiding messages because anybody can start counting letters. No, the strength of ELS codes is that they *authenticate* the identity of the messenger.

Rabbi ben Asher had said, "The secrets of the Torah are revealed in the skipping of the letters." Now what does that mean? That's an invitation to spend some time skipping letters. It was Dr. Gerald Schroeder, a world-famous nuclear physicist, who first showed me what I'm about to lay out here. Dr. Schroeder resides in Jerusalem, and I've had the privilege of spending Passover with him. We're good friends, and he was the one that showed me this, but it's common knowledge among serious Hebrew scholars.

While dedicated rabbis counted the letters carefully for years, we now have the number crunching power of computers at our disposal. I am grateful to mathematician Dr. Eliyahu Rips for the work he has done to reveal the words hidden in the Hebrew Scriptures.[41]

We find an interesting series of ELS codes from the very beginning of the Bible, starting in the first chapter of Genesis. Remember that Hebrew reads from right to left. The Hebrew word *Torah* – "law" – is made up of four letters, תורה, a *tau* (ת), *vav* (ו), *resh* (ר) and a *heh* (ה). These are the equivalent of our letters T O R H. Beginning in the first verse of Genesis in the Hebrew, we can count from the first t*au* (ת) 49 letters. Doing so brings us to a *vav* (ו). We then count another 49, which brings us to a *resh* (ר), and then another 49 letters brings us to *heh* (ה). In other words, counting the product of 7x7 systematically from the first word of Genesis spells out the word "Torah" in Hebrew.

Genesis

תורה = TORH

That might be a coincidence. There are just 22 letters in the Hebrew "alephbet," and it's not statistically inconceivable. We might find any number of words in Genesis by skipping letters. What starts to make us scratch our heads, however, is that we also find the letters T O R H by counting every 49 letters in the first chapter of Exodus. Once is interesting. Twice begs a closer look.

Exodus

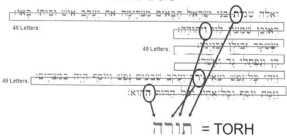

תורה = TORH

In Leviticus, we get a break, and we almost feel a sigh of relief rise inside us. Nor do we find T O R H in Numbers as we did in Genesis or Exodus. Well then, that seems to be the end of the matter – until we look even more closely. If we take a more careful consideration of Numbers, we find something startling. Counting every 49 letters gives us the word from back to front - ת - ו - ר - ה. There's still a 49-letter interval, but it spells T O R H backwards. In Deuteronomy, the same thing happens again! Again it spells Torah backwards (this time starting on the 5th verse, and including the 49th letter in the count).

Numbers

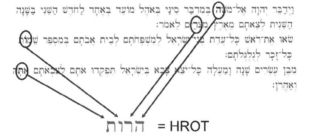

הרות = HROT

This no longer appears like mere coincidence. The word "Torah" is found spelled forward in Genesis and Exodus – at 49-letter intervals – and backwards in Numbers and Deuteronomy. When we reexamine Leviticus, we find something we didn't notice before. When we count by sevens – the square root of 49 – from the beginning of Leviticus, we find the interval of seven letters gives us the Hebrew word Yahweh[42] - יהוה - the I AM of the Burning Bush.

Leviticus

Intervals of 7:

These equidistant letter sequences do not just form words. They paint a picture. We see a design here: Genesis and Exodus spell "Torah" forwards, Numbers and Deuteronomy spell "Torah" backwards. In the four books together, the word *Torah* points to the name of God in the middle. The conclusion is that the Torah always points to יהוה - YHWH - the name of God.

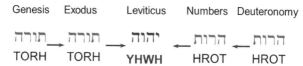

There is a great deal of significance in this discovery. If one letter is out of place, it all falls apart. It demands careful design, and it seems that when *Moses received the five books from God, the words were given to him letter by letter.* Remember, we are establishing the integrity of the Bible's design. We can do so through the multitude of prophecies throughout the Old Testament –

all of which point to Jesus. We can also find it in statistically improbable messages located within the very letters of the Hebrew text.

These ELS codes do not give us secret knowledge that's not found in the plain text of the Bible, and we should be wary of anybody trying to sell any ideas that can't be found in the plain-text. However, they do give us a perspective of God's foreknowledge. God knows what He's doing. They provide examples of His authentication, His thumbprint, so to speak.

In fact, it appears that Hebrew was designed to make this kind of wordplay possible. We hold in our hands a supernatural book, and the ELS codes offer yet another way to confirm that fact. The Bible was written by at least 40 authors over thousands of years, yet these revelations offer additional authentication that it came from outside our terrestrial environment, outside time. The Bible constantly tells history before it happens. When we discover that for ourselves, it changes our lives.

Judah and Tamar

Studying ELS codes doesn't just offer us clever little parlor tricks. They open to us validation of even the most puzzling Biblical passages. Consider the story of Judah and Tamar in Genesis 38. It's a strange story that explains the conception of Judah's surviving children – the ones who became the ancestors of the tribe of Judah. Yet, it's a dismal tale, and many people wonder why it's even in the Bible in the first place.

Judah's wife has died. His daughter-in-law married two of his sons, but they've both died in succession. Wearying of waiting for Judah to fulfill his promise and allow her to marry his third son, Tamar dresses up as a prostitute and tricks her father-in-law into sleeping with her. It's a sordid tale, yet it's a part of the genealogy of the Messiah. It's the kind of story we have trouble reading in the presence of other adults, let alone to small children.

Yet, we serve a God who has the power and grace to take even our brokenness and redeem it for His glory. We find in the genealogy of Christ not only the Tamar incident, but Rahab the harlot of Jericho, Ruth the Moabitess, and Bathsheba, with whom King David committed adultery. Despite the story's witness to human weakness, we can find the hand of God in the words of Genesis 38.

We also know that Jesus was born in Bethlehem. Why? Because King David's ancestors were from Bethlehem. We first find the value of that little town in the book of Ruth, in the story of Boaz, the kinsman redeemer of Ruth and Naomi. It turns out that when we look closely at Genesis 38, we find the name "Boaz" at 49-letter intervals, hidden centuries in advance. The name of Ruth is also there at 49-letter intervals. That could be considered a fun coincidence, except that the names of Obed, Jesse, and David also appear in that little chapter. The names associated with the family tree of David are all found at 49-letter intervals and in chronological order. That's astonishing, and it makes us realize that even when Saul was king, David was never an afterthought. The people begged for a king, and so God gave them Saul. However, God's intention was always to make David king. David was in the wings all along, and we find his ancestry encrypted in the 38th chapter of Genesis.

Take note. It's a long way from Genesis through Joshua and Judges until we meet David the shepherd boy in the seventh chapter of 2 Samuel. Yet, we find him nestled away in the letters of Genesis 38, always there in God's purposes and plans from the beginning.

Genesis 38

1 וַיְהִי֙ בָּעֵ֣ת הַהִ֔וא וַיֵּ֥רֶד יְהוּדָ֖ה מֵאֵ֣ת אֶחָ֑יו וַיֵּ֛ט עַד־אִ֥ישׁ עֲדֻלָּמִ֖י וּשְׁמ֥וֹ חִירָֽה:

2 וַיַּרְא־שָׁ֧ם יְהוּדָ֛ה בַּת־אִ֥ישׁ כְּנַעֲנִ֖י וּשְׁמ֣וֹ שׁ֑וּעַ וַיִּקָּחֶ֖הָ וַיָּבֹ֥א אֵלֶֽיהָ:

3 וַתַּ֖הַר וַתֵּ֣לֶד בֵּ֑ן וַיִּקְרָ֥א אֶת־שְׁמ֖וֹ עֵֽר:

4 וַתַּ֥הַר ע֖וֹד וַתֵּ֣לֶד בֵּ֑ן וַתִּקְרָ֥א אֶת־שְׁמ֖וֹ אוֹנָֽן:

5 וַתֹּ֤סֶף עוֹד֙ וַתֵּ֣לֶד בֵּ֔ן וַתִּקְרָ֥א אֶת־שְׁמ֖וֹ שֵׁלָ֑ה וְהָיָ֥ה בִכְזִ֖יב בְּלִדְתָּ֥הּ אֹתֽוֹ:

6 וַיִּקַּ֧ח יְהוּדָ֛ה אִשָּׁ֖ה לְעֵ֣ר בְּכוֹר֑וֹ וּשְׁמָ֖הּ תָּמָֽר:

7 וַיְהִ֗י עֵ֚ר בְּכ֣וֹר יְהוּדָ֔ה רַ֖ע בְּעֵינֵ֣י יְהוָ֑ה וַיְמִתֵ֖הוּ יְהוָֽה:

8 וַיֹּ֤אמֶר יְהוּדָה֙ לְאוֹנָ֔ן בֹּ֛א אֶל־אֵ֥שֶׁת אָחִ֖יךָ וְיַבֵּ֣ם אֹתָ֑הּ וְהָקֵ֥ם זֶ֖רַע לְאָחִֽיךָ:

9 וַיֵּ֣דַע אוֹנָ֔ן כִּ֛י לֹּ֥א ל֖וֹ יִהְיֶ֣ה הַזָּ֑רַע וְהָיָ֞ה אִם־בָּ֨א אֶל־אֵ֤שֶׁת אָחִיו֙ וְשִׁחֵ֣ת אַ֔רְצָה

לְבִלְתִּ֥י נְתָן־זֶ֖רַע לְאָחִֽיו:

10 וַיֵּ֛רַע בְּעֵינֵ֥י יְהוָ֖ה אֲשֶׁ֣ר עָשָׂ֑ה וַיָּ֖מֶת גַּם־אֹתֽוֹ:

11 וַיֹּ֣אמֶר יְהוּדָה֩ לְתָמָ֨ר כַּלָּת֜וֹ שְׁבִ֧י אַלְמָנָ֣ה בֵית־אָבִ֗יךְ עַד־יִגְדַּל֙ שֵׁלָ֣ה בְנִ֔י כִּ֣י

אָמַ֔ר פֶּן־יָמ֥וּת גַּם־ה֖וּא כְּאֶחָ֑יו וַתֵּ֣לֶךְ תָּמָ֔ר וַתֵּ֖שֶׁב בֵּ֥ית אָבִֽיהָ:

12 וַיִּרְבּוּ֙ הַיָּמִ֔ים וַתָּ֖מָת בַּת־שׁ֣וּעַ אֵֽשֶׁת־יְהוּדָ֑ה וַיִּנָּ֣חֶם יְהוּדָ֗ה וַיַּ֜עַל עַל־גֹּֽזְזֵ֤י צֹאנוֹ֙

ה֤וּא וְחִירָה֙ רֵעֵ֣הוּ הָעֲדֻלָּמִ֔י תִּמְנָֽתָה:

13 וַיֻּגַּ֥ד לְתָמָ֖ר לֵאמֹ֑ר הִנֵּ֥ה חָמִ֛יךְ עֹלֶ֥ה תִמְנָ֖תָה לָגֹ֥ז צֹאנֽוֹ:

14 וַתָּסַר֩ בִּגְדֵ֨י אַלְמְנוּתָ֜הּ מֵֽעָלֶ֗יהָ וַתְּכַ֤ס בַּצָּעִיף֙ וַתִּתְעַלָּ֔ף וַתֵּ֨שֶׁב֙ בְּפֶ֣תַח עֵינַ֔יִם

אֲשֶׁ֖ר עַל־דֶּ֣רֶךְ תִּמְנָ֑תָה כִּ֤י רָאֲתָה֙ כִּֽי־גָדַ֣ל שֵׁלָ֔ה וְהִ֕וא לֹֽא־נִתְּנָ֥ה ל֖וֹ לְאִשָּֽׁה:

15 וַיִּרְאֶ֣הָ יְהוּדָ֔ה וַֽיַּחְשְׁבֶ֖הָ לְזוֹנָ֑ה כִּ֥י כִסְּתָ֖ה פָּנֶֽיהָ:

16 וַיֵּ֨ט אֵלֶ֜יהָ אֶל־הַדֶּ֗רֶךְ וַיֹּ֨אמֶר֙ הָֽבָה־נָּא֙ אָב֣וֹא אֵלַ֔יִךְ כִּ֚י לֹ֣א יָדַ֔ע כִּ֥י כַלָּת֖וֹ

הִ֑וא וַתֹּ֨אמֶר֙ מַה־תִּתֶּן־לִ֔י כִּ֥י תָב֖וֹא אֵלָֽי:

17 וַיֹּ֕אמֶר אָנֹכִ֛י אֲשַׁלַּ֥ח גְּדִֽי־עִזִּ֖ים מִן־הַצֹּ֑אן וַתֹּ֕אמֶר אִם־תִּתֵּ֥ן עֵרָב֖וֹן עַ֥ד שָׁלְחֶֽךָ:

18 וַיֹּ֡אמֶר מָ֣ה הָֽעֵרָבוֹן֩ אֲשֶׁ֨ר אֶתֶּן־לָ֜ךְ וַתֹּ֗אמֶר חֹתָֽמְךָ֙ וּפְתִילֶ֔ךָ וּמַטְּךָ֖ אֲשֶׁ֣ר בְּיָדֶ֑ךָ

וַיִּתֶּן־לָ֛הּ וַיָּבֹ֥א אֵלֶ֖יהָ וַתַּ֥הַר לֽוֹ:

19 וַתָּ֣קָם וַתֵּ֔לֶךְ וַתָּ֥סַר צְעִיפָ֖הּ מֵֽעָלֶ֑יהָ וַתִּלְבַּ֖שׁ בִּגְדֵ֥י אַלְמְנוּתָֽהּ:

20 וַיִּשְׁלַ֨ח יְהוּדָ֜ה אֶת־גְּדִ֣י הָֽעִזִּ֗ים בְּיַד֙ רֵעֵ֣הוּ הָֽעֲדֻלָּמִ֔י לָקַ֥חַת הָעֵרָב֖וֹן מִיַּ֣ד

הָאִשָּׁ֑ה וְלֹ֖א מְצָאָֽהּ:

21 וַיִּשְׁאַ֞ל אֶת־אַנְשֵׁ֤י מְקֹמָהּ֙ לֵאמֹ֔ר אַיֵּ֧ה הַקְּדֵשָׁ֛ה הִ֥וא בָעֵינַ֖יִם עַל־הַדָּ֑רֶךְ וַיֹּ֣אמְר֔וּ

לֹא־הָיְתָ֥ה בָזֶ֖ה קְדֵשָֽׁה:

22 וַיָּ֙שָׁב֙ אֶל־יְהוּדָ֔ה וַיֹּ֖אמֶר לֹ֣א מְצָאתִ֑יהָ וְגַ֨ם אַנְשֵׁ֤י הַמָּקוֹם֙ אָֽמְר֔וּ לֹא־הָיְתָ֥ה

בָזֶ֖ה קְדֵשָֽׁה:

23 וַיֹּ֤אמֶר יְהוּדָה֙ תִּֽקַּֽח־לָ֔הּ פֶּ֖ן נִהְיֶ֣ה לָב֑וּז הִנֵּ֤ה שָׁלַ֙חְתִּי֙ הַגְּדִ֣י הַזֶּ֔ה וְאַתָּ֖ה לֹ֥א

מְצָאתָֽהּ:

24 וַיְהִ֣י כְּמִשְׁלֹ֣שׁ חֳדָשִׁ֗ים וַיֻּגַּ֨ד לִֽיהוּדָ֜ה לֵאמֹר֙ זָֽנְתָה֙ תָּמָ֣ר כַּלָּתֶ֔ךָ וְגַ֛ם הִנֵּ֥ה

הָרָ֖ה לִזְנוּנִ֑ים וַיֹּ֣אמֶר יְהוּדָ֔ה הֽוֹצִיא֖וּהָ וְתִשָּׂרֵֽף:

25 הִ֣וא מוּצֵ֗את וְהִ֨יא שָׁלְחָ֤ה אֶל־חָמִ֙יהָ֙ לֵאמֹ֔ר לְאִ֞ישׁ אֲשֶׁר־אֵ֣לֶּה לּ֔וֹ אָנֹכִ֖י הָרָ֑ה

וַתֹּ֙אמֶר֙ הַכֶּר־נָ֔א לְמִ֞י הַחֹתֶ֧מֶת וְהַפְּתִילִ֛ים וְהַמַּטֶּ֖ה הָאֵֽלֶּה:

26 וַיַּכֵּ֣ר יְהוּדָ֗ה וַיֹּ֙אמֶר֙ צָֽדְקָ֣ה מִמֶּ֔נִּי כִּֽי־עַל־כֵּ֥ן לֹא־נְתַתִּ֖יהָ לְשֵׁלָ֣ה בְנִ֑י וְלֹֽא־יָסַ֥ף

ע֖וֹד לְדַעְתָּֽהּ:

27 וַיְהִ֖י בְּעֵ֣ת לִדְתָּ֑הּ וְהִנֵּ֥ה תְאוֹמִ֖ים בְּבִטְנָֽהּ:

28 וַיְהִ֥י בְלִדְתָּ֖הּ וַיִּתֶּן־יָ֑ד וַתִּקַּ֣ח הַמְיַלֶּ֗דֶת וַתִּקְשֹׁ֨ר עַל־יָד֤וֹ שָׁנִי֙ לֵאמֹ֔ר זֶ֖ה יָצָ֥א

רִאשֹׁנָֽה:

29 וַיְהִ֣י כְּמֵשִׁ֣יב יָד֗וֹ וְהִנֵּה֙ יָצָ֣א אָחִ֔יו וַתֹּ֕אמֶר מַה־פָּרַ֖צְתָּ עָלֶ֣יךָ פָּ֑רֶץ וַיִּקְרָ֥א שְׁמ֖וֹ

פָּֽרֶץ:

30 וְאַחַר֙ יָצָ֣א אָחִ֔יו אֲשֶׁ֥ר עַל־יָד֖וֹ הַשָּׁנִ֑י וַיִּקְרָ֥א שְׁמ֖וֹ זָֽרַח ס

בֹעַז	Boaz
רוּת	Ruth
עֹבֵד	Obed
יִשַׁי	Yishay (Jesse)
דָוִד	David

בֹעַז	Boaz
רוּת	Ruth
עֹבֵד	Obed
יִשַׁי	Jesse
דָוִד	David

*All in 49-letter intervals; &
All in <u>chronological</u> order!*

Other ELS Codes

More than a century ago, Rabbi Samson Raphael Hirsch said, "The Jews' catechism is his calendar." The Jewish calendar is not just a series of bank holidays. The feasts of Israel are a yearly reminder of God's purposes and plans. Each feast has great meaning, put in place to teach prophetic events in advance. These appointed times were important to God from the very beginning:

Genesis 1:14 says:

And God said, Let there be lights in the firmament of the heaven to divide the day from the night; and let them be for signs, and for seasons, and for days, and years.

The word translated "seasons" here is המועדים - *HaMo'adim* - which means "the appointed times." The sun, moon and stars were put in place to help humanity keep track of these times, and there are 70 in total. There are 52 weekly Sabbaths each year. Passover Week includes seven feast days. Then there's *Shavuot* (Pentecost), *Yom Teruah* (Feast of Trumpets), *Yom Kippur* (Day of Atonement), and the seven days of *Sukkot* (Feast of Tabernacles). The end of *Sukkot* is celebrated by *Shemini Atzeret*, the eighth day assembly. When we add up *HaMo'adim*, we find a total of 70 days:

52 + 7 + 1 + 1 + 1 + 7 + 1 = 70

The number seven is central in the Jewish calendar. This seven-fold "heptadic" structure is evident in days, in weeks, in months and in years. We recognize that the week has seven days, and the seventh day is the Shabbat.[44] There's also a particular seven-week period – a week of weeks – at the end of which the Jews celebrate the feast of *Shavuot*, or Pentecost.[45] The religious year is a week of months, from the beginning of Passover in the month of Nisan to the end of the Feast of Tabernacles in the seventh month of Tishri.[46] The Mosaic Law institutes a week of years; it requires the Israelites to give the land a rest after each seven-year cycle.[47]

There is even a week of seven-year periods, a total of 49 years after which the nation is to celebrate a Jubilee year. The Law declares that on this 50th year, the Israelites are to forgive all debts. [48] In the Jubilee year, land returns to its original owners, and Israelites who have sold themselves into slavery are set free. God instituted a year, twice a century, when the people of Israel were given a clean slate. Peter uses the phrase "the time of restitution of all things."[49]

These appointed days were described in the Law by Moses, yet God foreordained them back at the very beginning when He created the heavens and the earth.

In Genesis 1:14, Moses writes about Creation and he tells us that God gave the lights of heaven for signs and seasons, for days and years. If we put the word *HaMo'adim* into an ELS computer search program, we find that it only appears once in the entire 32,000 words of Genesis. Just once. However, that one time is centered on Genesis 1:14 at intervals of 70 letters. It's remarkable that the word is located right there at the beginning, centered on Genesis 1:14 when God created the sun, moon and stars. It is even more remarkable that the interval is 70, when we know that there are 70 appointed times.

The text of Creation Week holds other encrypted mysteries. In the verses from Genesis 1:29 to 2:10 – in those few verses when Moses describes the creation of seed-bearing trees and plants – we find the names of over 25 trees and plants that are mentioned plainly elsewhere in the Bible. These include the tamarisk, terebinth, thicket, citron, acacia, almond, wheat, date palm, cedar, aloe, grape, boxthorn, cassia, poplar, pomegranate, gopher wood, thorn bush, olive, pistachio, hazel, fig, willow, oak, vine, barley, and chestnut. These appear encrypted both forward and backward by intervals from 2 up to 85.

Trees and Plants in Genesis 2

אשל	Tamarisk (2)	רמון	Pomegranate (8)
אלה	Terebinth, (-2)	נפר	Gopherwood or fir (8)
עבת	Thicket (or Dense forest) (-3)	סנה	Thornbush [*Crataegus*] (9)
הדר	Citron (-3)	זית	Olive (-9)
שטה	Acacia (-3)	בטן	Pistachio Nut (13)
שקד	Almond (5)	לוז	Hazel (-13)
חטה	Wheat (5)	תאנה	Fig (14)
תמר	Date Palm(5)	ערבה	Willow (-15)
ארז	Cedar (-5)	אלון	Oak (17)
אהלים	Aloe (6)	גפן	Vine (-18)
ענב	Grape (-6)	שערה	Barley (-28)
אטד	Boxthorn or Bramble (7)	ערמו	Chestnut (44)
קדה	Cassia (7)	לבנה	Poplar (-85)

We might think that words would show up just by statistical chance, but we find that's not so. Some words are not so easy to find. In fact, the word "Israel" occurs only twice in the first 10,000 letters of Genesis – at intervals of seven and fifteen. In other words, the name "Israel" has been searched for at letter intervals up to 100 – both forwards and backwards – and it only shows up twice. Yet we find the transliterations of Holocaust allusions scattered liberally in Deuteronomy: Hitler, Auschwitz, the Fuhrer, Eichmann, king of the Nazis, Germany, and Mein Kampf are encrypted in Hebrew letters.[50]

In 1994, researchers Doron Witzum, Eliyahu Rips, and Yoav Rosenberg caused a great uproar. The men had conceived of an experiment in the mid-1980s, the results of which they eventually submitted to a prestigious peer-reviewed journal called *Statistical Science.* In their experiment, they formed a list of 34 of the most prominent rabbis in Jewish history along with their dates of birth and death. Remarkably, each rabbi was found in the Bible encrypted with those dates of birth and death. The statistical likelihood of this taking place was about 1 in 775 million, but the statistical review board thought it was contrived. They said, "Let's add another 32 rabbis to your list." The researchers agreed and added 32 additional names, along with their dates of birth and death. These additional 32 were also found.

This, of course, created quite a stir. It was too bizarre to ignore, but the statisticians didn't want to have to deal with it. It took six years of back-and-forth reviews before the article was finally accepted for publication in 1994.[51]

After that, the big guns in cryptography got interested. The senior mathematician for the National Security Agency (NSA), Harold Gans, decided to do Bible ESL research on his own computer. He spent 440 hours of crunching the numbers over 19 days, and by the end of those 19 days, he concluded there was less than one chance in 62,500 that the codes were due to chance. He retired from the NSA and now teaches the Torah in Jerusalem. He ends a 1997 personal statement on the codes by saying, "After exhaustive analysis, I have reached the conclusion that the only information that can be derived from the codes discovered in Genesis is that they exist, and the probability that they are mere coincidence is vanishingly small."[52]

The Exploitation Begins

After this, Michael Drosnin famously published a book called *The Bible Code* in 1997. Many things in Drosnin's book are correct, but he also makes unwise arguments. For instance, he claims to have been able to use the ELS codes to predict the 1995 assassination of Israeli Prime Minister Yitzhak Rabin. He uses some contrived translations and suspicious mathematics, and his results are highly questionable. Harold Gans specifically commented against this sort of effort. In response to *The Bible Code*, Gans stated:

> The book states that the codes in the Torah can be used to predict future events. This is absolutely unfounded. There is no scientific or mathematical basis for such a statement, and the reasoning used to come to such a conclusion in the book is logically flawed.[53]

The ELS codes are useful for authenticating the design of the Bible. They should not and cannot be used to predict the future. Future-telling of this sort is called "divination", which the Bible strictly forbids.[54]

There are many decent books that give greater insight into the ELS codes. I would recommend Grant Jeffrey's 1997 *The Handwriting of God* [55] and his 2002 book *The Signature of God*.[56] Jeffrey

Satinover's 1997 book *Cracking the Bible Code* [57] and John Weldon's 1998 book *Decoding the Bible Code, Can We Trust the Message* are also worth reading.[58]

Of course, when we delve into this subject, the most important question of all is, "Does Jesus appear in the Torah's ELS codes?"

Chapter 7
The Yeshua Codes

Search the scriptures; for in them ye think
ye have eternal life: and they are they
which testify of me.

John 5:39

Then said I, Lo, I come (in the volume
of the book it is written of me,) to do thy
will, O God.

Hebrews 10:7

Rabbi Yacov Rambsel did ask the question, "What about Yeshua?" and he found a great many valuable treasures regarding Jesus in the Scriptures. Yacov and I became very good friends, and he made me aware of his provocative discoveries.[59]

Jesus told us plainly that the Scriptures spoke of Him, and we find this true through a multitude of Old Testament prophecies. We also find Him hidden in the text in a vast array of equidistant-letter-sequences. These ELS codes both validate the integrity of the Scriptures as well as continue to establish the identity of Jesus Christ.

It's important to note that the Hebrew name Yeshua is made up of four letters that have relatively high frequency: ישוע. It's not surprising, therefore, that the word Yeshua appears 5,538 times in the Old Testament, 2,919 going forward (136 with no intervals) and 2,619 going backward. The existence of those four letters isn't surprising, but we do find it interesting *where* the Lord's name shows up. We find Him in Genesis 1:1. We find Him again in Genesis 3:27 when Adam and Eve are covered, and there it says, "He will save." In the first chapter of Ruth, we find *Yeshua* at five-letter intervals, and in the famous 70 Weeks Prophecy of Daniel 9, we find *Yeshua* at 26-letter intervals. In the midst of many important prophecies throughout the Old Testament, we find the name of our Savior hidden in the letters.

Isaiah 53

Let's focus now on Isaiah 53 itself. We've spent a lot of time covering this amazing prophecy about the sacrificial death of our Lord. Let's take a moment to consider the words coded within the 15 short verses from Isaiah 52:13 to Isaiah 53:12.

• Yeshua is my name	ישוע שמי
• His Signature	מחתימו
• Messiah	משיח
• Nazarene	נזיר
• Galilee	גליל
• Shiloh	שילה
• Pharisee	פרוש
• Levites	לוים
• Caiaphas	כיפה
• Annas	ענן

- Passover — פסח
- The man Herod — איש הורד
- Wicked Caesar perish — קיסר עמל אכד
- The Evil Roman City — רע עיר רומי
- Let Him be cucified — יצלב
- Moriah — הירמ
- Cross — צלכ
- Pierce — דקר
- From the Atonement Lamb — מכפר טלא
- Bread — הלחם
- Wine — יין
- Obed — עבד
- Jesse — ישי
- Seed — זרע
- Water — מים
- Jonah — יונה
- The Disciples mourn — למדים אנן
- Peter — כפה
- Matthew — מחחי
- John — יוחנן
- Andrew — אנדרי
- Philip — פילף
- Thomas — תומא
- James — יעקב
- James — יעקב
- Simon — שמעון
- Thaddaeus — תדי
- Matthias — מתיה
- Mary — מרים
- Mary — מרים
- Mary — מרים
- Salome — שלמית
- Joseph — יוסף

We find more than 40 words and phrases associated with the crucifixion hidden amongst the letters of the Suffering Servant passage. We find the name of the high priest and the various elements of the Passover feast. We find the names of the disciples coded in Isaiah 52 and 53.

It gets even better. "James" isn't listed once, but twice, which is interesting because there were two disciples named James. Both James the son of Zebedee, brother of John, and James the son of Alphaeus would have witnessed the crucifixion of Jesus Christ.[60] The name "Mary" is encoded three times, along the woman Salome. One of the Marys was Jesus' own mother, but we also find Mary Magdalene and "the other Mary" involved personally in Christ's death.[61]

Any one of these names in isolation would not be particularly impressive. For instance, the name "Philip" is found 15 places elsewhere in Isaiah while the name "Thomas" shows up more than 200 times in Isaiah. The isolated appearance of any one name is not so important. We're interested in the ELS codes here because of the clustering of names all in one small location. There are more than 40 words relevant to the crucifixion of Christ densely encrypted in the 15 sentences of this passage. To suggest that this just happened by random chance denies the overwhelming strength of the evidence.

There are some interesting things to note. One of the three ELS codes for "Mary" is encrypted in such a way that it interweaves with "John." We find this significant when we recall that, while He was hanging on the cross, Jesus handed responsibility of His mother to His disciple, John.[62] What's more, all three sequences of "Mary" use the same letter *yod* that encodes the name "Yeshua."

What makes this clustering even more noteworthy are not just the many names present, but also the names that are *missing*. "James" is found twice, but it isn't found three times. The third James, the Lord's half-brother,[63] was apparently not present at the cross. Remember that Jesus' brothers didn't accept His authority until after the Resurrection.[64]

Notice who else is missing? Judas. The name "Judas" is made of high-frequency letters, but that doesn't appear to matter. The other 11 disciples are all listed, along with Matthias who was chosen to replace Judas, while Judas himself is strikingly omitted.

Incredible Design

Remember Ernest Vincent Wright's effort to write an entire book without using the letter E? Wright succeeded, but only after careful word sculpting. He took the most common letter in the English alphabet, and he tossed it out. His was a massively difficult job. He did it with great care and dedicated design. Consider another passage from the first chapter of his book:

> It is a story about a small town. It is not
> a gossipy yarn; nor is it a dry monotonous

account, full of such customary "fill-ins" as "romantic moonlight casting murky shadows down a long, winding country road." Nor will it say anything about twinklings lulling distant folds; robins caroling at twilight, nor any "warm glow of lamplight" from a cabin window. No. It is an account of up-and-going activity; a vivid portrayal of Youth as it is today; and a practical discarding of that worn-out notion that "a child don't know anything."

Wright did a fair job, and we applaud his effort. Even with all his skill, however, Wright's text seems cumbersome and difficult to follow. He had to leave out important, high-use words like *the, he, she, they, we, me,* and *them,* and some of his resulting sentences feel heavy and require a reread.

The books of the Bible demonstrate a similar, but far more involved kind of careful design. Every letter matters, just as Jesus warned. There's something extremely marvelous about the Bible's code that I don't want you to miss; God managed to space those letters without damaging the literary quality. The writing of the Bible is arguably the most beautiful in the ancient world. Isaiah's use of poetry is not awkward or sluggish; his book is recognized as an example of literary genius, even by secular readers. The fact that equidistant letter sequences pervade Isaiah 53 while it remains brilliantly well written should fill us with even greater appreciation and sense of awe for this precious gift God has given us.

The Bible codes are beyond any statistical explanation. As David Kashdan, Chairman of Harvard's Department of Mathematics said in 1996: "The phenomenon is real; what it means is up to the individual."

When people talk about the "Bible codes" they usually mean the equidistant letter sequences. There are a multitude of other kinds of hidden codes throughout the Bible, found in the form of types and prophecies, similes and symbols. The Bible is rich with hidden treasures for the cryptologist inside many of us, but it also communicates in straight forward, simple terms that even small children can understand. It is written for every one of us, whoever we are.

As we reach the end of this study, let us take a moment to set aside the controversies and sterile details and take a moment to reflect on the wonder of God's Word. Let us pause and stand in awe at the majesty of our inscrutable Lord. He's the God who created the universe in the first place, the God who chose to enter His own creation as a man and to fulfill our destiny for us. The phenomenon of the ELS codes is real, and what it means is up to the individual. Yet, I believe there's no way any of these hidden treasures could have been construed from inside our own time domain. They had to have been initiated outside of our four-dimensional space-time physical realm by a God who knows the end from the beginning and sees the purposes He intends to accomplish even thousands of years in advance.

I have mentioned a number of important books by other authors, and I owe a debt of gratitude to researchers like Grant Jeffrey and mathematicians like Harold Gan. I have gone into more depth in my book, *Cosmic Codes, Hidden Messages from the Edge of Eternity*, which we reprinted in 2004. It doesn't simply focus on the ELS codes but surveys the multitude of other codes – the microcodes and macrocodes throughout the Bible. The Bible has something for everybody, and God uses a great range of literary devices to communicate His purposes. Our job is simply to take the time to search them out. There are few revelations more exciting than finding something unexpected hidden in the pages of God's Word.

Let's bow our hearts for a word of prayer. Father, we thank you for Your Word. We stagger as we discover its nuances and the many ways that it points to Your wonderful creativity. You have given us an awesome treasure, and Father we ask that You will continue to open our hearts and lives through your Holy Spirit. May You do in us what You have done in Your Word, that we might be living and breathing representations of Your love and power and majesty, despite our many failings. By Your Spirit, help us begin to grasp the extremes You have gone to on our behalf. As we attempt to come to grips with Isaiah 53, we recognize the entire New Covenant is contained here, shouting from the Hebrew Scriptures centuries in advance. You have done so much for us — may we begin to appropriate the incredible blessings we received because You suffered so greatly. We thank You, and we commit ourselves into Your hands, with no reservation, in the name of Yeshua, Your Suffering Servant, and our Redeemer, Lord, and Coming King, indeed. Amen.

Endnotes

1   Thiele, E. (1983). *The Mysterious Numbers of the Hebrew Kings*, 3rd Ed. Grand Rapids: Zondervan/ Kregel, 217.

2   Clendenen, E. & Howard, J. (2015). *The Holman Illustrated Bible Commentary*. Nashville: Holman Reference, 710.

3   Matthew 8:14-17; Mark 15:28; Luke 22:35-37; John 12:37-41; Acts 8:26-35; Romans 10:16-21; 1 Peter 2:21-25. These are just the direct quotes of Isaiah 53 and do not include the many passages that describe Jesus fulfilling its prophecies. We will cover those in detail later in this book.

4   Retief, F.P. and Cilliers, L. (December, 2003). *The History and Pathology of Crucifixion.* South African Medical Journal: 93(12): 938–941.

5   As quoted in Allis, O. (1951). *The Unity of Isaiah. (A study in prophecy.)* (p. 2). Eugene, OR: Wipf and Stock.

6   Cf. Isaiah 13-24

7   Isaiah 13-14; 21:9; 39:1-8; 43:14; 47:1; 48:14, 20

8   Isaiah 45:6

9   See Allis, O. (1951). *The Unity of Isaiah. (A study in prophecy.)* (p. 40). Eugene, OR: Wipf and Stock. Allis does a thorough job of answering critics who deny a single authorship of Isaiah.

10 Allis, O. (1951). *The Unity of Isaiah. (A study in prophecy.)* (p. 40). Eugene, OR: Wipf and Stock. Allis does much better job of covering all these matters than I do in my little appendix jottings.

11 Isaiah 46:10

12 Josephus, F (AD 75). *The Wars of the Jews*. VI.5.2, VI.6.1, VII.1.1, and VII.5.2

13 Exodus 29:20-21; Leviticus 3:2-13, 4:17, 5:9, 7:2, 14:7, 16, 27, 51; Numbers 8:7, 18:17, 19:4, 18-19

14 Mark 6:4; John 7:5; Galatians 1:19

15 John 1:1-3; Philippians 2:10-11

16 Cf. Acts 14:8-10, 19:11-12, 28:8

17 2 Timothy 4:20

18 Matthew 26:62-63

19 Matthew 27:17-18, 23, 24; Luke 23:4, 14, 15, 22; John 18:38, 19:4

20 Matthew 27:16-26; Mark 15:7-15; Luke 23:17-25; John 18:39-40

21 Isaiah 41:8-14; 43:10-48; 44:1-6, 21-22

22 Bonar, A. (1852) *A Commentary on the Book of Leviticus*, 3rd Ed. (p.113ff). Dundee: James Nisbet and Co.

23 Matthew 8:20

24 John 13:27

25 Isaiah 59:3, 13-16; Jeremiah 8:5, 9:2-8

26 1 Peter 1:20; Revelation 13:8

27 Hebrews 12:2; Jude 1:24

28 Hebrews 10:1

29 Fulfilled in Matthew 26:14-15; 27:3-8

30 2 Timothy 3:16

31 John 15:26; 16:13-14

32 There is a play on the word for "branch" in Hebrew - *nazir* - which Matthew picks up on in Matthew 2:23

33 2 Peter 3:9

34 MacDonald's Idiomatic Translation (MIT).

35 Isaiah 34:4; Revelation 6:14

36 Isaiah 65:17; 2 Peter 3:13

37 See Hebrews 10:10-13; John 1:1-14; Colossians 1:13-19; Hebrews 1:1-14

38 Barrow, J. (2002). *The Constants of Nature: From Alpha to Omega – the numbers that encode the deepest secrets of the universe* (p. 142). New York: Pantheon Books.

39 Barrow, J. & Tipler, F. (1986): *The Anthropic Cosmological Principle.* Clarendon Press.

40 Wright, E. (1939) *Gadsby: (A Story of Over 50,000 Words Without Using the Letter "E")* (p.12-13). Los Angeles: Wetzel Publishing Co., Inc.

41 See also Jeffrey, G. (1997). *The Handwriting of God: Sacred Mysteries of the Bible.* Toronto, Ont.: Frontier Research Publications.

42 The true pronunciation of God's name is unknown. The rabbis considered it as too holy to speak out loud, and its correct pronunciation has been lost over time, and now YHWH is regarded as the unpronounceable name of God

43 Ruth 4:12

44 Leviticus 23:3

45 Leviticus 23:15-16

46 Leviticus 23:5; 23:39-43

47 Leviticus 25:4

48 Leviticus 25:8-13

49 Acts 3:21

50 Jeffrey, G. (1997). *The Handwriting of God: Sacred Mysteries of the Bible* (p. 113). Toronto, Ont.: Frontier Research Publications.

51 Witzum, D; Rips, E; Rosenberg, Y. (1994). Equidistant Letter Sequences in the Book of Genesis. Statistical Science, 9:429-438.

52 Hans, G (June 3, 1997). *Public Statement by Harold Gans.* Last accessed September 5, 2016 at http://www.torah-code.org/controversy/gans_statement.pdf.

53 *Ibid.*

54 Deuteronomy 18:10

55 Jeffrey, G. (1997). *The Handwriting of God: Sacred Mysteries of the Bible.* Toronto, Ont.: Frontier Research Publications.

56 Jeffrey, G. (2002). *The Signature of God.* WaterBrook Press.

57 Satinover, J (1997). *Cracking the Bible Code.* New York: Wm Morrow and Co.

58 Weldon, J. (1998) *Decoding the Bible Code - Can We Trust the Message.* Harvest House.

59 Grant Jeffrey and I are both indebted to Yacov Rambsel for his discoveries about Jesus in what we call the Yeshua Codes. Rambsel's discoveries are also explored in my 1998 book, *Cosmic Codes - Hidden Messages From the Edge of Eternity.*

60 Matthew 10:2-3

61 Matthew 27:61, 28:1

62 John 19:26-27

63 Mark 6:3

64 Mark 6:4; John 7:5; Galatians 1:19

About the Author

Chuck Missler
President/Founder,
Koinonia House

Chuck Missler was raised in Southern California.

Chuck demonstrated an aptitude for technical interests as a youth. He became a ham radio operator at age nine and started piloting airplanes as a teenager. While still in high school, Chuck built a digital computer in the family garage.

His plans to pursue a doctorate in electrical engineering at Stanford University were interrupted when he received a Congressional appointment to the United States Naval Academy at Annapolis. Graduating with honors, Chuck took his commission in the Air Force. After completing flight training, he met and married Nancy (who later founded The King's High Way ministry). Chuck joined the Missile Program and eventually became Branch Chief of the Department of Guided Missiles.

Chuck made the transition from the military to the private sector when he became a systems engineer with TRW, a large aerospace firm. He then went on to serve as a senior analyst with a non-profit think tank where he conducted projects for the intelligence community and the Department of Defense. During that time, Chuck earned a master's degree in engineering at UCLA, supplementing previous graduate work in applied mathematics, advanced statistics and information sciences.

Recruited into senior management at the Ford Motor Company in Dearborn, Michigan, Chuck established the first international computer network in 1966. He left Ford to start his own company, a computer network firm that was subsequently acquired by Automatic Data Processing (listed on the New York Stock Exchange) to become its Network Services Division.

As Chuck notes, his day of reckoning came in the early '90s when — as the result of a merger — he found himself the chairman and a major shareholder of a small, publicly owned development company known as Phoenix Group International. The firm established an $8 billion joint venture with the Soviet Union to supply personal computers to their 143,000 schools. Due to several unforeseen circumstances, the venture failed. The Misslers lost everything, including their home, automobiles and insurance.

It was during this difficult time that Chuck turned to God and the Bible. As a child he had developed an intense interest in the Bible; studying it became a favorite pastime. In the 1970s, while still in the corporate world, Chuck began leading weekly Bible studies at the 30,000 member Calvary Chapel Costa Mesa, in California. He and Nancy established Koinonia House in 1973, an organization devoted to encouraging people to study the Bible.

Chuck had enjoyed a longtime, personal relationship with Hal Lindsey, who upon hearing of Chuck's professional misfortune, convinced him that he could easily succeed as an independent author and speaker. Over the years, Chuck had developed a loyal following. (Through Doug Wetmore, head of the tape ministry of Firefighters for Christ, Chuck learned that over 7 million copies of his taped Bible studies were scattered throughout the world.) Koinonia House then became Chuck's full-time profession.

Learn the Bible

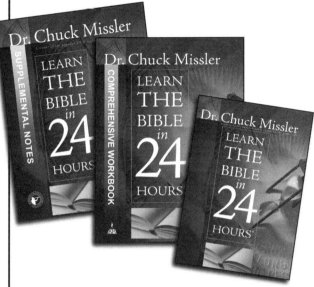

Are you ready for a detailed yet thoroughly enjoyable study of the most profound book ever written?

Using sound scientific facts, historical analysis, and Biblical narrative, acclaimed teacher Dr. Chuck Missler weaves together a rich tapestry of information—providing an accurate understanding of Scripture's relation to itself, to us and to the world at large.

Examine the heroic tales of Exodus, the lasting wisdom of Proverbs, or even the enigmatic imagery of Revelation with the simple, Scripturally sound insights and fresh perspectives found in *Learn the Bible in 24 Hours*. Whether you want to explore some of the less-discussed nuances of Scripture or you need a comprehensive refresher course on the Bible's themes and stories, *Learn the Bible in 24 Hours* is a great guide.

Hidden Treasures

For the novice as well as the sophisticate, this book is full of surprises. It includes subtle discoveries lying just "beneath" the text – hidden messages, encryptions, deliberate misspellings and other amendments to the text – that present implications beyond the immediate context, demonstrating a skillful design that has its origin from outside our space and time. Drawing upon over forty years of collecting, Chuck highlights in this book many of the precious nuggets that have become characteristic of his popular Bible studies around the world.

It is guaranteed to stimulate, provoke, and, hopefully, to disturb. It will confound the skeptic and encourage the believer. It is a "must read" for every thinking seeker of truth and serious inquirer of reality.